Shania Star
Whidbey Island
1998

ANGELA THE
UPSIDE-DOWN GIRL

〜〜 〜〜 〜〜 〜〜 〜〜 〜〜 〜〜 〜〜 〜〜

THE CONCORD LIBRARY

SERIES EDITOR: JOHN ELDER

Angela the Upside-Down Girl

AND OTHER DOMESTIC TRAVELS

\\\\\\ \\\\\\ \\\\\\ \\\\\\ \\\\\\ \\\\\\ \\\\\\ \\\\\\ \\\\\\

E M I L Y   H I E S T A N D

B E A C O N   P R E S S
B O S T O N

BEACON PRESS
25 Beacon Street
Boston, Massachusetts 02108-2892
www.beacon.org

Beacon Press books are published under the auspices of
the Unitarian Universalist Association of Congregations

"Maps" first appeared in an earlier form under the title "Atom City," in the *Boston Sunday Globe Magazine*.

"Hose" first appeared in *Jo's Girls: Tomboy Tales of High Adventure, True Grit, and Real Life*, edited by Christian McEwen, Beacon Press, 1996.

03 02 01 00 99 98   8 7 6 5 4 3 2 1

This book is printed on recycled acid-free paper that contains at least 20 percent
postconsumer waste amd meets the uncoated paper ANSI/NISO specifications for
permanence as revised in 1992.

Text design by Anne Chalmers
Composition by Wilsted & Taylor Publishing Services

Library of Congress Cataloging-in-Publication Data

Hiestand, Emily, 1947–
    Angela the upside-down girl : and other domestic travels / Emily Hiestand.
        p   cm. — (The Concord Library)
    Includes bibliographical references.
    ISBN 0-8070-7128-5 (cloth : acid-free paper)
    1. Hiestand, Emily, 1947– —Biography.   2. Women poets, American—
20th century—Biography.   3. Voyages and travels.   I. Title.   II. Series.
PS3558.1345Z465   1998
811'.54—dc21
[B]   97-52966

for my mother and father,
Frances Emily and Orris Sidney Hiestand,

and for Peter

For when the traveler returns from the mountain-slopes into the valley, he brings, not a handful of earth, unsayable to others, but instead some word he has gained. . . . Perhaps we are *here* in order to say: house, bridge, fountain, gate, pitcher, fruit-tree, window— . . .

—Rainer Maria Rilke,
Duino Elegies

Contents

Part One

ANGELA THE UPSIDE-DOWN GIRL

\\\\\   \\\\\   \\\\\   \\\\\   \\\\\   \\\\\   \\\\\   \\\\\   \\\\\

LIKE FLOTSAM jostled together, we had been drifting into our futures since morning in a Chevrolet Bel-Air, turquoise with vestigial tail fins. Judy's mother had loaned us the Bel-Air; Beverly was beautiful; and the fourth girl—we called ourselves girls—was already homesick. What was her name? Her drawing style was a pen-and-ink pointillism, thousands of dots with which she coaxed the illusion of realism from an atomized abstraction. It was nearly midnight when we entered the ambit of America's city on a hill. The first door we opened, on the outskirts of Boston, was the door to the Glo-Min Motor Inn, whose name took the *gloaming,* the old time of waxing shade, through the turnstile of American pop. In our room and presumably in all the rooms at the inn, the lamps, chairs, and television set were tethered to the floor by thick black chains, a look that might in later years be passed off as punk chic. Down the street a few blocks from the well-secured motel there was a late-night diner. We parked the Chevy outside, sat at the counter in a row, and ordered a dish called clam rolls.

It was the year that, longing for the Moon, four astronauts settled for getting back to Earth alive, the year that Cambodia was invaded, the year of Kent State. Our final senior project had been to protest, again, the war—draping the facade of our art school in sheets of black plastic which had billowed from the Doric columns like dark sails. In the diner now there was a local group, girls about our age whose territory was three booths along the windows—an expanse of plate glass alive with greenish fluorescence, with glints of chrome and reflected licks of fire from the grill. The girls eyed us for a while, then sent over a welcoming party, whose greeting, summarized, was what the hell were we were doing in their diner, and were we some "rich chicks cruising"?

The counter waitress told the girls to knock it off, and they did, but when we left the diner they followed, moving down the sidewalk after us, walking then running, a blade flashing just as we got the windows rolled up and the car doors locked.

That night of our arrival, by chance in one of the city's most insular, and soon to be embattled neighborhoods, New England was impression only: Squanto and Thanksgiving, Puritans in somber jerkins, some tea floating in the harbor. We had read *The Scarlet Letter* in high school, and once my Girl Scout troop had been taken by Greyhound bus as far north as New York City, where we saw *Camelot* and a delicatessen, events of equal splendor—the glistening white-gold stage and the glistening pickles and sodas of fabulous sorts (cream soda!), and metal trays hefting unknown salads, some of fishes and moist tentacles. From a harbor ferry, we saw the brawny goddess of Liberty wound in scarves of mist; we saw two tugboats bump into each other, heard the crews curse across the decks, and then the scout bus returned us to the east Tennessee hills.

Home was then Oak Ridge, and in that anomalous South of uranium and isotopes, with physicists and Danish Modern tapering about its living rooms, I felt none of the diffuse, bruised misgiving about the North that one could find, a century after Sherman, among many more Southern southerners. After high school I did not hesitate to migrate northward to a college of art in Philadelphia, the old city of the Atlantic Plain.

How lightly to me regional borders then signified: another new world could be chosen at a graduation party, with an offhand "Sure." Mark the logic that led four young artists to Boston: it was not New York, which Judy declared "too big," and it was not where any of us had come from. Ours was a tiny aperture of deliberation, and yet for me to aim at Boston was to travel farther north for a permanent dwelling than anyone in my family ever had — save for my great-grandfather's brother, Sam Callahan, who had adventured from Alabama to Alaska and frozen to death one winter on the Lonesome River, a fact pointed out to me by my Aunt Marguerite. Some members of our family had removed themselves from the Deep South and survived — some to Charleston, my parents as far north as Maryland — but none to Massachusetts, core of the Yankee mind. My maternal grandmother, Frances Webb Callahan Watkins, took the news as though I were bound on the first Arctic expedition.

The Glo-Min Motel was home for a week as the four of us hunted for a cheap apartment, by which we meant something so rock-bottom cheap that one aging real estate agent guffawed when he heard what we planned to spend.

"You girls could not be looking in a worse place," he then said cheerfully. "This is Newton. This is the completely wrong town for you." He unfolded a map and used a magic marker to cross off Newton and all the other professionally dappled neighborhoods, and also the ones he deemed too raw, which left only a few scattered patches. The one he said we must try was a community northeast of Boston, on the bay. "Winthrop" it said on the map alongside his large finger.

It has been a famous name in America since 1630, when, aboard the *Arbella*, John Winthrop delivered the sermon "A Model of Christian Charity" to the settlers preparing to make land. "We must," he said, "make each other's conditions our own, rejoice together, mourn together, labor and suffer together: always having before our eyes ... our community as members of the same body. . . . For we must consider that we shall be like a city upon a hill."

This set a tone—though we have learned to rue how many the Europeans' new world charity did not embrace, including the people whose name for themselves was the Massachusett. These centuries later, the Puritan covenant sounds to be a very call to tolerance and inclusion, the civil regard of souls, but it was, in truth, a compact for fierce conformity—that "same body" conceived in a narrow love that dealt harshly with anyone "contrarye minded." Still, we like these words of Winthrop, for they have slipped, as words will, the knot of their most local meaning, and have descended to us, have come down through the years as a kind of looking glass.

Fast strong currents swirl around the peninsula of Winthrop, and colonial oarsmen named the area Pullen Poynt. The peninsula was also secluded, and for a century, until the railroad came, it was a retreat with summer hotels and sailboats, white dresses and parasols. Winthrop's social climate had changed by the time we drove the Bel-Air into town, but the sea air was still refreshing, ten degrees cooler than Boston proper. The roses of Winthrop relish the town's salt atmosphere, climb its walls blousily, lay themselves down on the town's fences in blankets as thick as those garlanding the Derby winner. From the steep glacial hill in the center of town, the prospect sweeps down to mouse-gray sand and cord-grass marsh. Beneath its soft apron of mud, the marsh holds hen and wedge clams, with their china-white, spoon-shaped cavities, and quahogs whose shells once made the good purple wampum. Immediately back of the shorefront drive, along streets named Mermaid and Neptune, are rows of tidy summer cottages. But Shore Drive itself was then the tatty, transient part of town, a strip of former hotels turned into rooming houses and apartments with aluminum siding, or fake rock siding, the kind that resembles giant mixed nuts inexplicably plastered onto a wall. The air smelled of mollusk, salt, and rotting wrack. In some synaesthesia of the shore, coolness too was in the smell, and if the day was gray the place could feel like wet laundry.

My first home in New England was the second floor of a house on this strip, separated from the Atlantic by a seawall and a beach of coarse sand. The house was as little like a house by the sea as a house by the sea can be: it was dim and sour, with fuel-oil fumes crawling up the stairwell from the basement, with sheets of buckling woodgrain paneling, an omnivorous shag carpet, and overwrought iron and orange glass lighting fixtures—a knock-off travesty of Moorish lanterns—looping down from the ceilings. Impressively cheap, this house was also close by a station of the subway that could shoot us into the city, where we imagined that we would find jobs—jobs that for the moment were as invisible as the clams breathing under the glossy mudflats.

A popular job-hunting technique among art students at that

time was to put the finishing touch on a portfolio by wiping its pages with carbon tetrachloride—a carcinogenic fluid once used by dry cleaners. We bought a big brown bottle and swabbed the thin liquid over the acetate sleeves that held our artwork. The bright lakes of fluid evaporated instantly on the plastic, and were a completely gratuitous application, our petition to the commercial gods. Inevitably, the carbon tet sunk into the skin of our fingers and hands and its vapour came into our lungs, but that art was intimately bound with toxins we knew: our shelves were full of fixatives and toluene-borne sprays, killer colors like lamp black and all the cadmiums. For weeks we carried the immaculate portfolios along the streets of Boston's Back Bay, looking for our careers.

During that first year, when I was learning the cadences of New England and of adult work, my first true neighbor was the woman who lived on the first floor of the house on Shore Drive. Her name was Angela—Angela the Upside-Down Girl—and she was a famous stripper in a nightclub in the Combat Zone, a part of the city that has since been urban-planned away. Angela's stage name derived from her specialty, which was to completely strip while in a headstand. Offstage and right side up, Angela was a single mother with two children, a boy of about eleven and a girl of eight.

Many afternoons Angela's boy and I walked along the beach in front of the house on Shore Drive. He had very smooth skin and the plump oval shape of a seal, and he often wore a sweater without a shirt underneath—which made you think about the itchy fibers against his soft, mammalian skin. He spoke to me in a way no one his age has, before or since, as if I sorely needed instruction and he had that information. All forceful personalities could claim influence on my life at that time and I had never met such an assured boy, who seemed not quite a boy. The main thing that Angela's son wanted to impress upon me was the supreme importance of being, not earnest, but limber. "Limber" was the word he used, which he had learned from his mother. He had learned everything, he said, from his mother. Gymnastics were very important, he told me. He was studying gymnastics so he would be limber and flexible like his mother. Was I studying gymnastics? Had I when I was little? It was best to learn while still a child, but he thought it might not be too late.

The first time that I visited Angela's apartment was by chance; we needed to borrow a cup of something. "Sure, hon, come in." But before getting the flour or the sugar, Angela ushered me directly into her living room and gestured for me to sit on a furry white couch in front of the dominant feature of the room, which was an immense painting over the mantelpiece. The painting was done on a field of black velvet and portrayed Angela as reclining odalisque, naked save for a pair of red high heels and a diaphanous bit of veil over her arms. The painting had been a surprise, a gift from a group of admirers who had apparently modeled the pose after Ingres's languid, long-backed harem slave of 1894, the original of which hangs in the Louvre. I knew that painting, if only as a slide projected in the lecture hall. Whatever the painting on velvet lacked of Ingres's neoclassical technique—and in truth, that might be all—it made up for in palpable presence. It was a good likeness and there was no doubt that it was Angela, perhaps an Angela of ten years earlier. Other than the black background and red shoes, the colors were pinks and white-pinks, less pearly than those of Ingres, and instead of his blue satin drapery and peacock feather fan,

9

a bamboo leaf motif played over two sides like a vignetting fringe. Around the painting was a frame of black enameled wood, and around the frame was a string of miniature colored Christmas tree lights.

Angela told me that she did not turn on the Christmas tree lights except on special occasions, one of which was now. She waited until her guest was seated in the living room in front of the painting and then snapped on the lights so one could appreciate the change in the overall effect. It was a good overall effect *before* the lights were switched on, and with them — "Boy, oh boy" and "Holy cow" are things people might have said, if they could think of anything to say at all.

Angela loved the painting, and though one can imagine a child psychologist's unsmiling caveats, I think her kids did too. What was it but the image of the body that kept their lives together, that made their home, that generated food and clothes and heat, that made their universe spin? The emblem ornamented by lights over the hearth was, like its patrician cousins, plainly a shrine to the lady of the house, here Aphrodite as working woman. As with all shrines, there was an inevitable distance between the image and the belief it embodied. None of us is identical with our bodies, and Angela was not one with the body in the painting, and so she was free to look on it as she did — with pride and detachment, as when a magnate gazes at a picture of his fortunate manufactory, or a captain on a rendering of a favorite sloop.

Never once did Angela refer to herself as a stripper, but always as a gymnast or gymnastic dancer. The club, she explained, was the best place for a gymnastic dancer to earn steady money, which steady money affirmed the central mythos of her household: that to be limber and gymnastic is a powerful tool, a ticket in this

world, like math or grammar. "Have you had any gymnastic training?" she asked me the first time we had coffee. Like her son, Angela looked sad when I said that I had not. Being tear-gassed in protest marches, lied to by Presidents, and seeing a city burn for a
prophet's death had been one kind of education, but none of that
was yet knowledge of what could make Angela say, "It's a good job,
hon. I'm the headliner."

One day Angela issued me an invitation, the first formal social
invitation I would receive in New England. My roommates and I
and our dates were to be her guests at the club where she was the
star performer. She would like us to come Saturday night for the
main show at ten o'clock. We arrived at the club a little early, as Angela had asked us to, and she came out from her dressing room and
introduced us to the club manager, who was gruff in a not-
avuncular but just plain gruff way. Angela also introduced us to the
bartender, to one of the other performers, and later, during her act,
pointed us out to the other customers as "my neighbors, who are
just out of school." I saw that we were a novelty mix of mascot and
country mice, that we were bits of paint on Angela's palette that
night, adding to her star, and I felt confused and glad. She was, I believe, on the verge of asking us to stand up and say where we came
from, like visitors to a new church.

For her act, Angela wore a lime-green and black costume, net
stockings, and elbow-length lime-green evening gloves — apparel
of a splendor greatly beyond (as was one Hester Prynne's) and yet of
considerably less coverage than that approved by what Hawthorne
called the "sumptuary regulations of the colony." There was a jazz
drummer who played while Angela performed, and some music on
a record player. The runway was set behind the bar and elevated, so
that the audience looked up slightly to Angela's body.

Outside the club it was August; when we had arrived the heat of

11

the day was just giving way as a tangy fog drifted in from the sea and settled into the canyon close of the city's sheer, high walls. Inside, the club was air-conditioned, smoky, chromed and mirrored, and jammed with middle-aged men in sports shirts. Angela was completely at home upside down, rock-steady during the whole act: rising swiftly into a headstand, bumping to the drum, slowly pulling off her stockings one by one, then unzipping her costume and somehow removing it too. There were spangled pasties on her breasts, with long beads that hung down toward her face. I remember thinking, as everyone must have, a good deal about *how* she was accomplishing the whole thing. It seemed a foregone conclusion that she would be both upside down and naked at some point, but how this would actually occur was a source less of erotic tease than of sheer logistical drama and suspense.

Even though she was a pro, one worried for Angela the whole time, the way one does for a tightrope walker at the circus: Would she lose her balance? Would she manage zipper and garter snaps? For this line of work, Angela was no longer young; she was already half the soft, lined roué, and to engage in a nightly drama to defeat gravity was not merely a career-extending technique but a production that touched and tickled her audiences. At some moment in her act one could feel the tenor of the room shifting, the audience aware of another pitch. I won't insist that it was art with a capital A, but it was something rather like it. She was not so much a transcendentalist pointing to an ideal beyond the world of experience, as she was an inversionist, transforming by reversals within the all too real. Do I navigate the fine line about this life? It was hard, and redolent of limitation, but of little she made much. The applause started even before she had finished her routine, and when she threw out the final bit of apparel—two thin boas that had been coiled around her arms—that was the finale, and the middle-aged men in sports shirts stood up and cheered.

After her act, Angela had drinks sent to us on the house, whatever we wanted. The star came by our table and flirted with our boyfriends. She stayed in character all the while she was at the club; she was none of the other Angelas I had seen—in her kitchen boiling spaghetti, on the seawall smoking, at the door bundling her daughter for school. She was only the exotic gymnast of the Kit Kat Club whose name appeared on a sign in the window—not only the A, but *all* of the letters of her name scarlet letters, with flourishes of gold sparkles for shadows. The headliner may have seemed to some a woman whose career was a deviant offense to the moral order. But the ground of the city on the hill had thawed some since Hawthorne worried about idealism calcified, about the dark side of a high moral vision. It had room for Angela, although it did ask her, like the refractory beauty of old, to dwell apart, and by the sea on a margin of town.

As our boyfriends flirted back with Angela, they wavered between gallantry and sophomoric humor, an awkward blend that they could not quite master. Angela was unfazed; she addressed the boyfriends like downy teenagers, then shared a laugh with them like *flaneurs* and compatriots of the demi-monde, then commanded the hushed attention due a grande dame. We were guests in her salon, and when we left in the early morning she saw us to the door, beyond which stood a bouncer in an electric-blue suit, and she blew us kisses. The light over the door of the club was yellow, and the neon of the blinking club sign was purple, and these two complementary colors pulsed alternately over our faces while we stood in the entrance saying good-night. Then we walked out into a thin fog that diffused the lights of the clubs and caused their hot pinks, blues, and yellows to seep into the moist gray air as watercolors seep into prepared paper.

A few weeks later, someone in our house awoke in the middle of the night, startled by sound. Rising from her bed, she walked down the hall to a row of windows, outside of which there lay a rustling black sea and a party of carousing teenagers, boys and girls dancing on the wide seawall. A radio was playing—it sounded like a song about saying good-bye to rubies and days. The tide was coming in, beginning to break over a clump of boulders, and there was a fetid salt smell from the beds of knotted wrack that blanketed the beach, each tangle fixed to its rock by a simple holdfast. A fingernail clipping of moon floated just inches above the waterline, a snip about to slide away. Threading the hallway to the window, the person had guessed—and now as she looked out on the night she was really sure—that she had no idea what place this might be. Her body, too, was unfamiliar, not unappealing, only unknown: a form into which she had recently arrived, from where she could not say. There was no name to call herself. The clock hands said the hour, but not a year. The suspended woman stood long at the window, unafraid but feeling entirely stripped, outside time and space. Was the sea the same sea? How had she arrived here, to see a night brawling by a body of water? What rooms had led to this window? And why such a monstrous lamp on the ceiling?

DRIVE

\\\\\\   \\\\\\   \\\\

Vitis rotundifolia is the southern muscadine, the scupper-nong, whose grapes are made into jam and jelly, sometimes into a straw-colored wine that a woman might keep in a special bottle and bring out to share with a granddaughter home from a date. The scuppernong vine on the land on the Crescent Ridge of Alabama is a lavish festooning old thing with scruffy yellow-green leaves bigger than most hands, and, at this time of year, in early summer, heavy with clusters of hard green grapes. The great plant is the sort of detail that would have mattered to my Aunt Nan Dean—a woman who liked her stories laced with detail, and who was particular about the particulars, selecting and shaping raw reality until her stories were, as they say in today's gyms, buffed.

One of her stories involved this very vine: its unripe, green grapes; a brother who had been warned not to eat them; also a deity with an omniscient eye; and, to thwart the latter, a thick cotton quilt. (If the story was a moral fable, and it surely was, what was that delight the teller took in the boy's doomed play with the great eye?)

Most of a century later, my cousin Nancy and I are standing by the scuppernong, which is today supported by four slender pillars

15

of poured concrete, a testament to our Uncle Will and his belief in the infinite possibilities of cement. Looking down through a slope of cedars, oaks, and pines, we can see a painted brick bungalow with a porch that runs across the whole facade. Through the trees, we can also make out the bed of river pebbles that form the driveway where our aunt parked her 1957 Buick sedan.

Nan Dean Blackman was a delicate woman, and a Buick sedan of the late 1950s was a full-size American car from the era when "car" meant two or more tons of heavy-gauge rolled steel. Encased in that robust carapace, Nan Dean looked especially fragile, an appearance that made her driving technique all the more surprising to the uninitiated.

"You rode with her more often," I say. "How would you describe it?"

By "it" I mean the unique motion of a car when that hummingbird took the wheel. My cousin, who is a person of tact and accuracy, reflects.

"I believe," she says carefully, "that the word would be *lunge*."

The lunging journeys of Aunt Nan Dean's car began when she eased the sedan down her driveway and poked the nose of the car out onto the Crescent Ridge Road, a wide, fast road by the late fifties, but one that Nan Dean and her sister Frances, my grandmother, could remember as a footpath through their father's farm, and later as a narrow dirt road, so dry and powdery that any passing vehicle raised a cloud of clay dust—like a veil, the women said. Nan Dean always paused for a moment on the lip of her driveway (traffic could come *flying* over the crest of the hill) and then she pressed down with all her strength on the gas pedal.

Bamm! The Buick shot forward like a racehorse out of the gate and continued briskly for a hundred yards on the mighty pulse of gas. But no sooner was the car underway than Nan Dean removed her foot entirely from the gas pedal, and so directly the Buick began to glide, to go slowly and yet more slowly until, just before the car reached stasis, our aunt, or sometimes a passenger, declared, "It's giving out!"

At that—and with the expression of urging on an inexplicably dawdling child— Nan Dean administered another full-force shot to the accelerator, really stomping on the pedal this time to indelibly impress upon the car the concept of forward motion. As the Buick lunged forward again passengers were bolted to the backs of their seats. I liked that. I remember thinking it must be like the G-force we were just beginning to hear about.

⫴ ⫴ ⫴

She was born Nancy Dean Callahan on the 23rd of August in 1892 in Greene County, Alabama—the fifth of the thirteen Callahan children, one of my four aunts (technically, my great-aunts, but as both of my parents were only children, their aunts and uncles did double-duty). Aunt Nan Dean lived to be a hundred, and she first learned to drive in 1934, when she was, as my mother's people say, "a full adult." At a time when cars were still scarce, and when most Southern women still relied on male kin to carry them places, Nan Dean wanted to drive her own car. She got to do so in part because her husband, her senior by ten years, declined to take on the automobile. Which was curious because Arthur Blackman was mechanically gifted. He had studied engineering, was involved in building complex machines for producing paper bags, but the man had some profound resistance to the dawning automotive age. "Everybody," our cousin Bill Johnson remembers, "tried to get Arthur to drive, but they couldn't do it."

And Uncle Arthur did not absolutely need to drive. For some years he worked at what was called "the furnace"—the iron foundry at Holt, owned by Central Iron & Coal—and later he took a job at the paper mill situated on the banks of the Warrior River. Arthur could get to either the furnace or the mill by bus, or by accepting rides with fellow workers. Church was less than a mile away. The horseshoe pit was a two-minute walk across the road, on Temo and Marguerite's land. It was Nan Dean who needed to travel to variable and distant places, transporting many kinds of cargo and persons from here to there along her fluxing, self-made route. So in 1934 she bought a secondhand four-door Chevrolet, and asked Sister Faith's boy, Bill, to teach her to drive it.

It was not surprising that Aunt Nan Dean wanted to drive herself, nor that she would refer to it as "setting out"—a phrase that both she and my grandmother used to convey more sense of purpose than merely "going out." Nan Dean had first, famously, set out in 1895, at age three. Six of the thirteen Callahan children had been born by that time, and all of them, including the baby, John Newman, were dressed each Sunday morning in a scene that grown-up siblings invariably invoked by the word "melée." On one such morning, when Nan Dean was the last child to be bathed and dressed, the little girl grew weary of waiting and began to hop about her mother asking, "Mama, what am I going to wear? What am I going to wear, Mama? Mama, what dress am I going to wear?"

It was a predictive, not merely petulant question, for Nan Dean would grow into a woman who might have invented fashion had it not already existed. In her wedding portrait she wears a gown with the elegant drape of a Chanel (she made it); her upswept hair holds a pearl comb; her dark almond eyes are serene; and the picture, which must have been made in a commercial photo studio in downtown Tuscaloosa, conveys the general effect of a Venetian principessa. Given her flair for clothing the body, and the fashion pronouncements she issued her sisters in adulthood, it is all the more evidence of Nan Dean's innate desire to set out that, on that particular melée morning, when her overwhelmed mother replied, "Nancy Dean, I do not care what you wear, you can go to church naked," the infant Nan Dean did.

My grandmother especially liked to tell the story: "And so, precious, your Aunt Nan Dean struck out. She *flew* out of the door, naked as a jaybird, and was half a mile down the road without the first stitch before Brother Will caught up with her and brought her back home and we got her dressed." ("Naked as a jay bird" was the phrase I could not tire of hearing, having the jay tendency myself, and being intrigued by the suggestion that jaybirds are more naked than other birds, even the *most* naked of creatures.)

Setting out, then, was in Nan Dean's nature, but in the thirties learning to drive was daunting. As I recall, learning to drive in the 1960s still offered up drama (the dreaded parallel parking), but in 1934 the car was a true primitive. Power-assisted and rack-and-pinion steering were unknown; gears were manual, suspensions bouncy, and there was a monster clutch. A driver needed muscle to brake, and upper-body strength to steer. The sprite Nan Dean must supply heavy torque—turning and turning the wheel—merely to control one of the stubborn young driving machines along the dirt roads of a rural county. In that era, driving—and learning to drive—called for complete concentration. Complicating the project was the fact that Bill Johnson, the instructor, was a very young man at the time, whereas his aunt was already A Known Force.

Still savoring his triumph, the Bill of eighty-two years opens with a précis of his pupil: "Let's just get Nan Dean's background real fast. Did you know that she had the water put out there?" By "out there" Bill means beyond the city limits, where the Callahans lived on fifty country acres adjoining the farm of Osceala and Lena Keene. "She had the electricity brought out there. She had the first telephone put out there. She had the bus put out there, and got the bus schedules made so that her husband could get to work and back. She had the Crescent Ridge Road paved. She *did.* She would go into the Power Company, or the Telephone Company—went right inside after the head knocker. She negotiated with them about the water, the electricity, the telephone, and it got to where when she went in one of those offices, everybody scattered. I carried her there before she could drive, and saw her in, and when she came out she'd tell me what had happened. Oh Lord, yes, she told me. It was going to be done—they may think they're not going to do it, but they *are.* The first thing she had done was the water."

Bill asks me, "Do you remember the porcelain pedestal lavatory sink that was in Aunt Nan Dean's bathroom? Well, that came out of a men's barber shop. She found it at Oviatt Bowers's junkyard. This was before she had a car and I carried her everywhere. I will bet you I made six trips down there to that junkyard about that pedestal lavatory. I can't remember the price, but let's say that Bowers wanted fifteen dollars. Nan Dean said five. She just kept going back to see him, and she explained to him, 'Mr. Bowers,' she said, 'no one, *no one* in Tuscaloosa County has a bathroom big as mine that can handle that sink. And you are not going to get rid of it except for me.' One day I drove her there again, and Bowers saw her coming and he was worn out. Said, 'Good Lord, Miz Blackman,' he said, 'take the thing!' And she said to me, 'Quick, Bill, get't and put't in the car.' And—I know you remember this—if Nan Dean sat next to you, I don't care where, if she was talking and you didn't listen to her, she reached over and got a *pinch* of you.

"Okay, that was Nan Dean. And so when she wanted to learn to drive the car, she wanted to tell *you* how to do it! Temo tried, and several of them tried, and they just came to *noo-ooo*. They gave up. Finally I was the only one left. She came to me and I told her, 'Aunt Nan Dean, this is your last chance.'" Bill's voice grows resolute, swells, the tone of an old soldier with a war story.

"I said, 'Aunt Nan Dean, nobody else is going teach you but me. And *I* am going run it. *You* are not going to say a word. And you are *not* going to pinch me.' I said, 'You have got to *promise*.' She promised, and so I carried her over to the Keenes' road because there weren't but two houses there. I explained what each thing on the car was. I explained how you crank it, put the clutch in, slip it in low, take your foot off the gas, put your foot on the clutch, put the brake on, stop. Up and down that road for a week, and finally, on the seventh day" (here I expected Bill to say "I rested") "finally on the seventh day, I said, 'Aunt Nan Dean, you know everything I know.'"

After this transfer of knowledge, the young man went on to other life achievements—building industrial plants in Panama was one—while Aunt Nan Dean continued to drive for forty years and, as Bill says, "never had a wreck or even scratched that car."

Once our Aunt Nan Dean had arranged for all the major utilities to be done satisfactorily, she set out for the offices of the

Tuscaloosa News, where she spoke sternly with the editor-in-chief about the copy errors staining his pages—a conversation that resulted in "Mrs. A. W. Blackman, Proofreader," a position she held for many years. Another day, her destination was the main department store in town, where she informed the executive manager that the timing of his store sales and advertisements was "pretty bad."

"Ma'am?" the man sniffed.

Nan Dean reasoned for him. "Mr. Sanford," she said, "the paper mill is the biggest operation in town and has the biggest payroll. You mustn't *have* a sale except the day after payday at the paper mill."

"We hadn't thought about that, Miz Blackman. We appreciate it. We'll do it."

⑊⑊⑊   ⑊⑊⑊   ⑊⑊⑊

Good as she was at it, municipal infrastructure was only a related sideline to Nan Dean's principal lifework—which was Hostess To A Lot Of Tuscaloosa County. And in retrospect, it is possible to guess that her driving style was due in large part to this primary calling; that it was less a forgetting to keep her foot on the gas pedal than the assigning of this minor detail of life's motion to a properly subordinate place. I mean she had a lot of other stuff to do in her car than just drive it. While the engine of the Chevy (and later, the Buick) was near idle much of time, the mind guiding the car was in rapid motion, attending to the mysterious rules of the road, of course, but moreoever to her passengers—who were what if not *guests* in her mobile parlor?

As Hostess of the Buick, Nan Dean must ensure that everyone had a nice seat, that the wind was not blowing anyone's hairdo to

smithereens, that there was enough air—and above all, that everyone in her car was having a good time. To that end, she launched
conversation and steered it along hopeful lines. As a very young
woman Nan Dean had read an anonymous Victorian essay enti-
tled "The Four Leaf Clover" and had committed its verities to
memory. The four leaves of the clover were faith, hope, love, and
luck, and all were important—though, of the leaf of hope, the
nameless author had written, "Without hope we would not be
strong enough to follow this earthly path. Hope emits to all a
brighter ray."

The brighter ray was great in Nan Dean, and its pulse tempted
her to arrange others into brighter, more hopeful forms—"whether
they needed it or not," one of her brothers observed. Her vehicles
for reform included the standard luncheons and showers, but also
evening card games under the ceiling fans (bridge or hearts, no
poker), and camps along the creek bank, and tableaux in which
campers got themselves up as scenes from silent movies. She won
me and my brothers over with her watermelon picnics, seed spit-
ting allowed.

Nan Dean's only child, a son, came in for much improving attention of course, and whatever that was like for him, it produced a
princely man. She watched closely over the deportment (as it was
then called) and education of a boy who was known as a youth for
heroic tantrums, later for uncommon decency, for wide-ranging
acumen, and for engineering waterworks in the Israeli desert—
and she watched over many other children too. "Every *one* of us,"
says my mother, "who went to the university were housed by her at
some time. We could have called that house the Hotel Nan Dean."

By the time my generation came along, she was at the
height of her powers. ("She had had more time to practice *being*

Nan Dean," my cousin notes.) One of my earliest dining memories dates to the large table of the Hotel Nan Dean, where for dessert my aunt served something that was, as she explained to me, the solid food of the ancient gods, the anointing oil for their locks and raiment. It was Nan Dean's favorite dessert, and it was called *ambrosia*.

I was stunned, deeply disappointed, to learn that what immortals prefer to eat above all else is oranges slices with shredded coconut on top. (When presumably they could have anything they wanted.) At six, in a metal glider on the porch, watching fireflies swim in the gray-green aquarium of an Alabama dusk, I thought we were closer to an elixir when Uncle Arthur brought out a half-gallon of ice cream from the Piggly-Wiggly. Gradually, though, I came to understand that for Nan Dean, ambrosia, the dessert, was as much rite as taste, that she prized the ambrosial in its many forms, and that above all she knew that it was—with repeated trips to the Power Company—within our grasp.

"I have something to show you," she whispered one day the year I was seven or eight, in Alabama for summer vacation. Beginning a ritual that lasted well into my adulthood, she hopped to the top rung of her stepping-stool and opened a high cupboard door. She reached into the cupboard with both hands, drew out a dark red glass object, and held it, hovering, just over my head. Was there always sunlight piercing the glass, whirling dots of ruby through the room, or did that happen only once? Only once, of course, but the object overhead did routinely have on me the general effect of stained-glass windows on the faithful.

"This," my aunt always announced, "is a ruby glass vase. Now ruby glass," she continued, "is a very fine glass—made from *pure gold*—and I'm keeping this for you. This vase will be yours when I die."

She then returned the ruby glass vase to the cupboard, hopped down to the floor, was satisfied, and continued on her path. I remained stock still, alone in her kitchen, which had returned to normal as though a small red miracle had not just hovered in the air, as though I deserved something to be held for me, as though gold could be made into glass, as though Aunt Nan Dean *were* going to die. I got to be almost sanguine, though, about the ruby future that depended on a death—partly, I think, because as my aunt pronounced "die," with an extra syllable and a springy uplift at the end (like a fancy ice-skating jump), the word suggested not a mournful event, but a rather enticing activity. Also, I had no desire for the vase itself. I wanted only its color.

On other occasions, my aunt called me into her bedroom where she sat in a silk slip powdering herself at a kidney-shaped table—a "vanity" she explained, as the surrounding air filled with a small cumulus of powder. (Here we will skip over the hours I spent baffled by the word "vanity," which was—how could this be?— both a very bad thing, an actual sin, and a gorgeous piece of furniture.) An ornate box of powder occupied the center of the vanity, just as a nearly identical box did in my grandmother's bedchamber. In that time and place powder was an indispensable part of a woman's toilette, and I doubt that my aunts and grandmother ever went out into their own kitchens and parlors—let alone into the larger world—without first powdering their faces. Their powder boxes were not the disposable cardboard boxes of today's dusting powder (if you can even find it) but sturdy wooden caskets with hinged lids that held tinted engravings under a piece of glass. The engravings were of off-duty shepherdesses dressed like opera divas at the Met, swinging on garlands or fanning themselves—images migrated to a rural Southern county from Versailles, another world that thoroughly powdered itself. The powder inside the boxes was a kind called "loose," and when touched it was cool, with the plumpness of sifted flour, and it could not be molded into any fixed form.

Once Aunt Nan Dean drove her Buick as far as our home in Tennessee and stayed for two weeks. I was eight or nine then and she was to sleep in my room, in the other twin bed, a daring arrangement presented to me as fun. Upon arrival, my aunt hung two weeks' worth of dresses in my closet and then she opened up her valise—a stout brown case with two thin gold bands and a cowhide handle—and released a platoon of bottles, jars, tubes of unguents, lotions, cremes, and talcs across my dresser. As Aunt Nan Dean advanced her troops, my dresser (site of a plastic statue of Trigger, a skate key, and not much else) began to look like the cosmetic counter at Loveman's Department Store. As I stared, my aunt pointed out that none of the potions were cucumber-scented.

"I loathe cucumber," she told me confidentially, blithely excommunicating that mild innocent of vegetables. I did like cucumber, but it was a dazzling moment for me, child of the house of reason and tolerance, to witness an adult being unabashedly nonrational. Cucumber was out. Don't give her any cucumber soap, ever. Nothing cucumber. My aunt then reached into a pocket of her valise and drew out a gift for me. The package was sensational—a slender thing with a clear plastic lid—but I had no idea why I might need a set of guest towels. A mental lacuna that was, no doubt, just what Nan Dean was planning to remedy.

"Thank you," I said.

And then night fell, and it came to pass that my Aunt Nan Dean snored. She snored undeniably. She snored loudly and in a regular rhythm. She snored in a sound like a valve gurgling in a swimming pool—a sound that would have pretty well completely deconstructed (had deconstruction then existed) the whole concept "lady." But in 1956 I only knew that to report my aunt's grizzled sawing to anyone, alive or dead, would be an act far far worse than snoring itself. Actually, even if deconstruction had existed, and even more improbably, had been introduced into our household or any household on our street, it would have lasted exactly as long as it would have taken a mother to say "If you ever sass me or your father like that again, you are going to have no allowance for a year—do you understand me?" How did a child of the fifties feel about adults and everything they did and said? Respectful, that's what. They were The Adults, they were In Charge. This idea constituted the whole, quaint, iron-clad plan of my youth. And so Nan Dean's secret was completely, utterly, entirely safe with me for many many decades. For forty-two years. Even now I am going back and forth about this detail, and am going to leave it in only as proof against gilding.

⫿⫿⫿ ⫿⫿⫿ ⫿⫿⫿

"Was she a pioneer, then, as a Southern lady driving a car in the 1930s?"

"Ooouuuweee," Bill Johnson answers, making the long drawn out sound that my grandmother made too, a musical sound that has in it pleasure, admiration, and a measure of raised eyebrow. "Ooouuuweee, I guess she was. Yes, if it had been today, she would have been one of those fem—, one of those fem— . . ."

He can't say the word.

"*Yeah!*" he says finally. "She would have been right up front."

Even when young, I understood that Aunt Nan Dean's brothers and sisters were amused by her, and also that their sister's actions would not have been considered especially amusing if performed by a man. Older, I also understood that although any man with Nan Dean's tendencies would have promptly been run for county commissioner or state legislator, unless he was very talented and skillful indeed he would not there have enjoyed the range and influence Nan Dean forged in her unofficial realm.

Nan Dean Blackman's genius was to at once embody and subvert prevailing conventions of Southern womanhood. In this task she had company in my grandmother, a woman who rode horseback and who, in her wedding vows of 1915, omitted the standard word "obey." My grandmother was also gifted at living, but her approach differed from Nan Dean's. Indeed, during nine decades together these two sisters sustained a strong, subterranean debate, the overt subjects of which included: Was it was proper for a man, specifically my Grandfather Foster, to do the grocery shopping? Who had most closely mastered their mother's biscuit recipe? Which was the finest soap opera, "As the World Turns" or "The Secret Storm"?

All hard questions, but only proxies for a larger debate. Nan Dean's aim in life was action, and my grandmother's was the paradoxical action-through-non-action of mystics, and so against the field of sisterly devotion there could often be felt trace battles of an unresolved polarity.

"Do you recall when Nan Dean decided to do a history of the Holt Baptist Church?" my mother asked me recently. "She went to your grandmother and said, 'Frances, I'm going to write the history of the church and I want *you* to do it with me.' Well, Mama wasn't interested in doing a history, but she didn't come out and say no. It happened then that Nan Dean often came across the road to Mama's house with the history, bustling with tasks for Mama. Mama said, 'Um hmmm, Um hmmm,' but she never performed any of the tasks. Finally Nan Dean finished the history by herself but named Mother as one of the authors and put Mama's picture in the front along with her own picture. When the book came out, there was a current picture of Mother, looking old and *wrung*, side by side with a gorgeous picture of Nan Dean taken decades earlier. What is it psychology calls it—passive aggression? Mother practiced *that* when she needed to, whereas Nan Dean practiced the regular active type."

|||| |||| ||||

A child could easily feel the sadness that settled into the bungalow house after Uncle Arthur's stroke, how hushed it was in the room where he lay, a drawn figure in striped pajamas who sometimes tried to speak in an alien, garbled voice—which when I think about now makes tears come to my eyes and makes me wish I had been wise and had known to just go over and kiss him, but then only made me shrink from the dark room in terror. She, of course, would not hear of her husband living anywhere but home, and nursed him for years, and learned to decipher his eerie new tongue.

One morning several decades after her husband's death, Aunt Nan Dean suddenly began to talk with me about Arthur as a young man, recalling his quick, mischievous wit. "Oh, he was a big tease," she said. "Although," she added, "after the time in 1912, he got solemn."

She was very old that morning in her sunroom as we sat together on her wrought-iron divan, and when I asked, "What happened that year?" she was gone, was on the Atlantic Coastline Railroad, taking the train to Alabama from Florida where Arthur had found work.

"I was coming home that day to have my first baby," she said, "but during the layover at the Jacksonville depot I started to faint. I lay down for a minute, and I must have looked so pale that the nurse's aide—all the big stations had a nurse's aide in those days—the nurse's aide called an ambulance and the railroad doctor."

When the ambulance arrived, Nan Dean protested; more precisely, she threw a hissy-fit, at least as much of one as a fainting woman could throw. "Oh, but I *must* get on the train," she cried, and tried to push past the doctor. "I must go home! They are *expecting* me. Let me on the train! I *must* go."

"You know me," she said, sliding back into the present to pinch me. "I'll *go* if I'd die on the train!"

And then she only remembers a nurse plaiting her long hair and laying it on a hospital pillow, and a doctor saying the word "toxemia," and then . . .

"My baby had been buried a good little while before I regained consciousness anymore. I have never known," she said, "and you need not ask because I was unconscious long after the baby was born—I have never known whether the convulsions killed the baby, convulsed him, or whether the doctor ended him."

A few years later, her second child, a girl, fell ill and died at one year and four months. Of that time, Nan Dean said simply, "I was whipped down then."

She let me see a little that morning into her especial motion—how the losses had first unnerved her, dimmed her birthright of energy, and then slowly intensified her measure of life, even as young men may return from war prizing breath itself, even as the old, scarifying initiation rites of tribes throughout the world gave their young the certain knowledge that being itself is the glory, that what Nan Dean called "go" shames the ever-present shadow. She did go on, but she was not, of course, unscathed. The losses left her fiery, and also anxious, aware that kindness is no special protection. Some of her stream of talk was surely to fill the silences in her world, and some of her going was to sidestep whatever came to her in stillness. "Just look at them," I overheard her huffing once, in indignation, and in longing, as my grandfather strolled slowly across his yard to join his wife in their garden. "They're never apart."

⫿⫿⫿   ⫿⫿⫿   ⫿⫿⫿

"I have some electrical work," she said into the telephone. It was Christmastime then. She was eighty-five, summoning a man over to change a lightbulb in her front hallway, but that was not new, she had always considered installing a lightbulb a job for a trained electrician.

"Let me," I said.

"Do you have a *license?*" she inquired.

And she got out the quarter she would give the master electrician, the major electrical contractor who personally handled her lightbulb work. My grandmother's house must have been full that year, for my husband and I were staying in Nan Dean's back bedroom. Late Christmas night, long after the platters and chocolate cups were back in the sideboard, long after everyone was sound asleep, he and I were awakened by a resonant, high-pitched sound.

Two o'clock, said the radium-tipped hands, and we slipped out of bed and down the long hall. The front parlor was dark save for a single lamp spilling its light onto an old old woman at her piano, singing, and not quietly, but really leaning into it through a sleepless night.

"Bringing in the sheaves," she sang. "Bringing in the sheaves. We shall come rejoicing . . ."

llll llll llll

When, at ninety-something, Nan Dean left her bungalow to live in a nursing home, the removal was, as it must often be, a reluctant journey. The home was a one-story red brick building on a knoll. There were hickory rockers on the porch, and the staff were kind and good, but only the most oblivious would not feel the narrowing, the leveling of those rooms. As the props of her world dissolved, however, Nan Dean did not—which for anyone in any of America's nursing homes, has to be counted among life's top feats. She dressed in fine lingerie; she offered you tea, and overlooked that there was none on hand. She attracted a beau about whom she was clear-headed. "Well, he's not worth much," she said, gesturing at the man in a wheelchair going by her door, "but he *is* sweet on me." And she took the occasion of a slow decline to roam, ever more freely, the landscape of memory—the great memories, of marriages, births, and deaths. And particulars. Whatever Brother Will said, their mother had chestnut-red hair. "Not red-red," she said, pulling me close, "chestnut-red."

llll llll llll

There is no point, however, in denying the fact that there was genuine danger in Nan Dean's driving style, and that some of her relatives, who will remain anonymous, avoided her car if at all possible. Says one, who loved her, "I was sure that she would run off the county bridge several times. You know she liked to *talk* while she was driving, and she liked to look you right in the face when she talked, and so she was scarcely ever looking at the road."

It's so. Why, then, my cousin Nancy and I now wonder, did no one—neither of us, no other member of our family, no neighbor, no state trooper—offer our aunt a word of reform, a syllable of caution, about her driving?

The reason that comes to us as we are looking at the river pebbles through the oaks, is a tautology, the logic of which must often be the preferred kind for speaking of souls, each one true by definition. This is what we said: No one tried to improve Nan Dean because Nan Dean was someone you did not try to improve.

"Ooouuueee," Bill will say later near this spot, fingering the clay ground lightly with a walking stick, watchful for the fire ants that ripple across the ground like stinging jewels. "That is exactly true."

M A P S

‖‖   ‖‖   ‖‖

People think they're very close to the answer, but I don't
think so. . . . Whether or not nature has an ultimate, simple,
unified, beautiful form is an open question.

—Richard Feynman

DURING THE 1950s, our family traveled frequently between the Atomic Age and the Age of Mule Agriculture, a journey
we accomplished by piling into my father's Chrysler and driving
three hundred miles from our home in Oak Ridge, Tennessee, to
the land of my many relatives in Tuscaloosa County. Motoring on
two-lane highways, in a blue car with three children in the back
seat, the trip took nine hours. To the naked eye, it was standard fifties road fare—with "Are we there yet?" and "Boys, stop tickling
your sister"—and perhaps the roads of that America were full of
people like us, trying to draw a map between an agrarian past and a
technological future.

Our journey began in a town built in secrecy and haste, in
a remote fold between the Cumberland and Smoky Mountain
ranges, a place that for more than a decade after its creation did
not appear on any but the most occult maps. The Black Oak and
Chestnut ridges had once belonged to the Cherokee Nation,

and then to Scots-Irish settlers who had come to the secluded hills and valleys of east Tennessee with their north-country ballads, recipes for clear whisky, and tales of devils invited in to eat apple dumplings as big as fists. The landscape was also what a handful of federal agents were seeking in 1942: a sparsely populated place, not far from a rail line, close to the clean waters of the Clinch River and the vast new TVA lakes.

There were three hypothetical schemes for the mission to be attempted in this quasi-wilderness, each so tenuous and unfounded as to sound like fantasy. But in an action characteristic of the entire undertaking, the directors of the Manhattan Project decided against testing these schemes in advance (no time, they felt) and called for a ferociously expensive plant to be built for *each* of the unproven techniques. These colossi, along with a research laboratory, were given the code names that I would hear throughout my childhood; K-25, Y-12, and X-10—names that my brothers and I would say as easily as we said Tonto, cat's eyes, and Fudgesicle. One plant held the calutron, an electromagnetic device made of a vacuum chamber and ten-thousand-ton magnets coiled round with silver from Fort Knox. In another there was a cascading arrangement of microscopic filters through which molecules of a corrosive gas were passing one by one. People who were there when the plants got underway remember that K-25 emitted a deep hum along its length, a sound like a hive of bees preparing to swarm.

In August of 1945, a wristwatch was found in the debris of Hiroshima. It is an old-fashioned watch with a round face, and although it is very badly burned, the hands of the watch are still readable, stopped at 8:16 A.M. Only after that hour, an hour which began to alter our idea of time itself, did most of the workers in the foothills learn what they had been doing. In the secret plants, physicists, engineers, industrialists, and busloads of young women from the east Tennessee countryside had separated enough U-235, a rare isotope of uranium, to provide the fissionable matter for the atomic bomb named Little Boy.

〣〣 〣〣 〣〣

My father and mother arrived two years later, when my father took a job lawyering for the Atomic Energy Commission, the new agency formed to manage the atom. There were other job offers for a young veteran and legal scholar who had been editor of his law review, but this one appealed most to a couple of modest means, with a newborn baby, largely because the job came with a house. It was a plain "C-style" house — one of the eight pre-fab patterns for the instant town — and it was built of cemesto board, which was a novel sandwich of cement and asbestos. In September of 1947, when my parents arrived in a green Ford, the gates to Atom City were still guarded night and day by armed sentinels. My mother and father had clearance passes, and I was waved in with them, two months old, asleep on the back seat.

My hometown would struggle, one of the managers wrote in his memoirs, to keep up with the military's eagerness for the gray-black powder called enriched uranium. After the war, the fact that nuclear weapons work was performed at Oak Ridge was not itself a secret, but the how-to for separating uranium was intensely guarded information, so the doings and even the purpose of the plants were seldom discussed socially, and never mentioned to children. The people of our town, like Americans elsewhere, then believed in the promise of the atom, and in the story that the new weapons were a deterrent. But why would you mention to a child turning five, wearing a shiny pointed hat and dazed by a cake and its candles, that the island of Elugelab in the Marshalls had just been vaporized by the first thermonuclear bomb? And so my brothers and I, and Christine Barnes, Amanda, and the Nelson twins, all of the kids on Gordon Road, grew up thinking of the unseen plants only as the mysterious places where the energy that was "too cheap to meter" came from.

That was the hope in those days, when the atomic scientists — many of whom had petitioned Truman not to use their brainchild on the innocents of a city (demonstrate it in a deserted place, they had urged) — longed for some redemption. In that first decade of the nuclear age, official language focused on the possibilities of plentiful energy, on radioisotopes for healing the body. Everyone likes to point to the latter program, an unequivocal good which made a menu of isotopes available for medicine and research — including californium-252, so useful in cancer therapy. The scientists of Oak Ridge also did work on bone-marrow transplants, on energy conservation, and on the messenger RNA. They made boxes for the moon rocks. And so well did the atoms-for-peace part of the story obscure the other part that I had been active in nuclear disarmament campaigns for years before I understood that I was working to end one primary, bread-and-butter activity of my hometown.

Today, although the enrichment process has shifted to other sites, Oak Ridge is still the home of Y-12, the nation's largest storehouse of weapons-grade uranium, and to Oak Ridge National Laboratory. The town's culture has changed, of course, since the 1950s. The Department of Energy has opened old files (thank you, Hazel O'Leary), and the town has recently installed a Japanese temple bell cast especially for Atom City by a master bellmaker of Kyoto. Soutetsu Iwazawa remembers that in Japan during the war, many ancient bells were melted down to make weapons, and he said that for this bell he would like to reverse the process.

We will need all forms of imagination to reverse the effects of decades of nuclear weapons manufacturing. Today, anyone can drive a few miles out of my hometown through one of the prettiest woods on earth, turn onto a narrow paved road on the side of a ridge, and look out on what locals call simply "the barrels"—acres of steel drums stacked several high, squatting on the flatland as far as the eye can see, each drum filled with some low-level stew of radwaste and chemical toxins, hot rags, wrenches, liquids—the containers "like nothing else in Tennessee," as Wallace Stevens once said, contemplating the curious jar of human ordering. This is the site of the old K-25 gaseous diffusion plant, and estimates to clean it up run into the hundreds of billions of dollars. Too much for government these days, and the current plan is to invite bids from private contractors. How long will it take?

"I don't think any one knows," one DOE official in Oak Ridge tells me with a candid sigh. "It will just be years and years."

This town in Tennessee, so steeped in the specific hopes and horrors of this century, is also for me the landscape of simple affection that each of us must have, the one lodged so deeply it lies in the body's memory. Once, when I had returned to my first home after thirty years of northward migrations and stood at the base of the hill up Georgia Avenue, the door of time opened suddenly wide, with no warning, and I was trudging up that hill carrying a cabbage for my mother: in the body itself, in its muscles and limbs arose the exact feeling of that walk, fresh and complete; in the body the feel of the dense cabbage in my arms; in the body the contour of the hill, and the fall later, on the path, blood and gravel mixed in my knee, the scar that formed. I cannot say how old I was that day, but young enough that I had mistaken the cabbage for a lettuce, which is what my mother had sent me for.

"Up and at 'em, Atom City!" the radio deejay called each morning. As a young man, my father disappeared each weekday morning into a building called the Castle—plain-vanilla barracks architecture, but labyrinthine, atop a hill, and as well protected as any medieval castle. Only adults with clearance passes could go beyond the lobby, and so that was the feature I knew best, especially the olive-green floor. Many afternoons I sat on a bench waiting for my father, watching the janitor wax the floor with a round machine that moved over the linoleum like a serene, blind animal. The security officer might tease me: "You could discover secrets in there," he said one day, nodding to the closed door.

I often tried to imagine the interior rooms where my father did law—arranging for the millions of troy ounces of silver to be returned to Fort Knox; telling some Strangelove project directors that no, it was definitely not legal for them to sell a herd of accidentally irradiated pigs on the Tennessee livestock market; investigating the plutonium fire at Rocky Flats; and always being so scrupulous and Dust Bowl–boy honest that he would not bring home so much as a pencil from his office. "That's government property, kids" he explained. A patient man in the bureaucratic vineyard, called "the peacemaker" by his colleagues, the first of my civics teachers and the only one who taught me how to fish.

Our town was then a kind of modern frontier village, insular and close, full of purpose and people pulling together, like immigrants to a new land. The day that my brother Andy, perhaps four, tired of coloring the disciples, wandered out of Sunday school, and started walking along the turnpike, he was scooped up in only a few blocks: "Aren't you Sparks Hiestand's little boy? Let's get you home." When not in school my brothers and I were rustling on feral quests along the namesake ridge of our town—and when night closed around us we were at home in its shadows and folds. The town that cradled the abyss also gave us that—a voluptuous ease and comfort in the night, in its loamy, porous smells; its grays, green-blacks, and slates; its shards of light through ink-dark hydrangeas. On Halloween eve, all the front doors of Atom City opened for us; voices in the doorways admired our pumpkin heads and black capes, large hands came toward us dropping popcorn balls into our brown paper grocery-store bags. And each ordinary day, Monday through Friday, someone called "He's home!" the moment one of us saw our father walking over the hill onto our street. I hold these few simple things to the center of remembrance to say that the atomic town had many things in common with other villages.

But only ours was the home of "the technological fix"—that phrase that would shimmer over years like a promissory note, the phrase coined by Dicky Weinberg's father, who was a physicist. How we liked that word "physicist," because it began in delight with "fizz" and had buzzy, hissy sounds, and because to be a physicist then in Oak Ridge was to be a local god. In such a town, the school science fairs were the *festas* of our culture. By junior high, a good science project was a route to popularity—"Did you see DeDe's magnet experiment!!"—and for several summers beginning when my best friend Ellen Jane and I were eight, we were overjoyed to be drafted into a real-life research project.

The lab at X-10 was investigating sources of cold light, and scientists there had the idea to enlist children to collect the common lightning bug needed for some of the experiments. They paid us a penny a bug—which sum amazed and conflicted us, because we caught fireflies anyway, for fun (that quick lunge at a wink of light, and with luck your palm closes around a fluttering, ticklish set of wings), and we would have given our catch to science for free. Many nights we slept next to our jarred *Lampyridae*, the creatures exuding their acrid smell, weakly lighting up the books on our nightstands: *The Mystery of the Brass-Bound Trunk, The Secret of the Old Clock*, stories of the girl sleuth who could locate secret passageways, could save the innocent who faces ruin if the mystery isn't solved.

Childhood in Atom City had the usual amount of making things out of gimp (lanyards for some reason), and afternoons at Clue, as Mrs. White committed murder or Colonel Mustard did. Ellen Jane and I had skate keys permanently slung around our necks on worn grosgrain ribbons, but we must have been among the only girls on earth who went regularly to the Atoms for Peace Museum to practice being nuclear engineers: slipping our hands into sets of lead-lined gloves, manipulating the bright fuel rods of a simulated graphite reactor, saying out loud the words "fission," "fusion," "critical mass." After practice, we entered the theatre of the silver Van de Graaff dome, a large generator on a pedestal—a demonstration of static electricity. The man tending the generator spoke seriously for few minutes about "a force that could kill a person," then beckoned a child onto the platform, toward the quiescent silver dome.

"Go on, honey. It's all right."

So you took a breath, put the palm of your hand on the cool dome, and then your hair began to stand straight up like the quills of a porcupine on alert, or those of a spiny urchin. It was funny; it was hilarious, and Ellen Jane and I began to call it "doing the dome." (Early geek chic.) Other days we skated to the shoe store to slip our feet into the fluoroscope and stare at the bones of our feet. This metal device, which resembled the combined fortune-telling machine and scale outside the grocery store, was an X-ray tube with a fluorescent screen at one end and an eyepiece at the other. Any body part placed between the tube and the screen produced a clear image, even in a lit room, and for a few years before it was quietly pulled out of the stores, the fluoroscope—which, of course, gave off a slug of radiation—was considered the ultra-scientific way to size a shoe to a child's foot.

We were modern. We knew the terms "heavy water," "abstract expression," "jet engines." We said, "See ya later, alligator." We understood that the future was going to be spotless, that energy would flow like golden rain over the earth, bringing a peace and level of comfort never before known. No teacher had to urge us; on our own we pored over the periodic table, memorizing rare earths and noble gases, the atomic weights of argon, europium, molybdenum, xenon, and zinc. The atom was our turf—as native to us as steel to Pittsburgh, cheese to the village of Brie—and it was perhaps inevitable that we would make an important discovery.

It happened the summer we were nine, smitten with the card game canasta. Lying on our stomachs making melds, we noticed that if we stared very hard at the frozen discard pile, at the Cumberlands out the picture window, at the Zenith, even at our own arms, we could see minute transparent vibrations. Everywhere. Neither specks nor particles, these looked to be more like the spaces humming between things, the medium in which grains of the known were sliding around, attracting and repelling one another. What was happening? Were our own eyes like electron microscopes? Were we seeing into "the very structure of the universe"? We had no way to test our discovery, and no one we told seemed to recognize its significance (so often the case in major breakthroughs). But we did not forget about the dancing transparency. In hindsight, I think I'll claim that we had arrived at a primitive, homespun version of modern string theory—the idea that each of the fundamental particles is generated by an infinitesimal "string" of pure energy, each of which has a particular pitch, a generative vibration.

The canasta discovery was surprising—less because we were nine-year-olds whose background in physics was listening to jokes about the half-life of the neutrino at our parents' cocktail parties than because, at that date, the only model of the atom we had seen was the atom as tiny solar system: the pop-icon atom with a central nucleus circled by electron planets in shapely orbits. That was the folk atom sewn on our swim-team patches, printed in maroon on our school notebooks, and engraved on the town seal. It was also the inspiration for the full-figured atom we saw one evening near dusk: a plump man tossing hard candies into the crowd from a float. His head, encased in a round mask like a diving helmet, was the nucleus, and the electron rings were hula hoops looped around his body, bobbing as he danced—the whole effect less like an atom than a sabled snowflake or lanky spider. But then what *did* atoms look like? It was the same question that the nuclear physicists were asking. Theoretically, the solar system model had collapsed long before it was being sewn onto our swimsuits, and the "basic building block" idea was giving way to the slippery house of quarks—to mesons, partons, gluons, to particles named color, charm, and top quark, all entities with only a tendency to exist.

At nine and ten and eleven, Ellen Jane and I simply assumed that the true atomic structure, when found, would be a kind of Rosetta Stone for our lives, would clarify the jumbled macroscopic world, too—terrifying piano recitals, the need for starchier crinolines, the sad madwoman who lived on Indian Lane, the little wars crackling on the radio news, a place called Cyprus, my tragically straight hair. Scientists, I later learned, were divided on this point: some dismissed such extrapolation as a naive overinterpretation of the very specific atomic realm. Others went much further than we had—speculating, for example, that free will might be beholden to the uncertainty principle.

Though I had embraced the atom as a boss metaphor and sciency little pal, I knew—we all knew—that it was also more swift and terrible than lightning. How did we know? No child of Oak Ridge had yet seen the images of Hiroshima and Nagasaki, pictures that operate on us now with the force of the sacred. But our elders had. And some of them had witnessed Trinity, and the thermonuclear tests, and one day the hands that had placed the sphere of plutonium into the case of the Fat Man bomb would place a dinner plate in front of me, touch my shoulder kindly.

Not for many years would we read the eyewitness descriptions, but some sense of what our elders had seen and felt had already transferred to us—in the way they spoke, I suppose, tones of voice, in their eyes, in sentences interrupted, also in the evacuation drills, marches down a dirt road into nowhere, the cognitive dissonance of ducking and covering, the idea that desks that did not stop spit-balls would shield us from "the flash" at the window. Don't look, the teacher said. And so when I did read the accounts, I felt the for-mal pain so exactly described by Emily Dickinson — "The Nerves sit ceremonious" she wrote — but I was not surprised to hear how the cold of early morning went blindingly bright and hot with a light that "bored its way right through you"; how the *Journada del Muerta* desert was filled with luminescent purples, with a thick parasol of spectral blue, swirls of flame, a ball of fire that grew and rolled, that kept coming and coming, one man said, closer; how the path of the shock waves was visible through the morning clouds; how a thunder kept echoing back and forth across the des-ert floor.

⑊ ⑊ ⑊

Our town was also a normal American town in having the normal amount of denial about these weapons. (Even now, they come and go in the national conscience, and it proves hard to hold in mind how they are real, in real places: 2,850 of them in New Mexico, 2,000 in Georgia, 455 in Louisiana; 12,500 in all, each one geometrically crueler than Little Boy, many loaded and un-loaded at the "hot cargo pad" at Albuquerque Airport and trans-ported along Interstate 40.) But it is undeniable that our normal town, one ground-zero of the techno-future, was in many ways nothing like its nearest neighbor, the hamlet of Oliver Springs, where a turkey shoot was held each Saturday morning — which did not mean, our father explained, shooting *at* turkeys but at targets *for* turkeys, which were the prizes. It was unlike the nearby towns of Clinton and Sevierville, the old east Tennessee towns where the yards were animated by ceramic elves and cobalt-blue gazing balls, and also unlike the genteel Upper South of Chattanooga and Memphis.

Growing out of none of these earlier realities, our town was a spaceship landed, not very softly, in an alfalfa or tobacco field. And what did the older Tennessees think about Atom City? Many of the families who had been removed from their lands by eminent domain were understandably bitter. Other natives were merely worried and skeptical. When Cas Walker, who sponsored the TV show with the local singers Bonnie Lou and Bester, campaigned against fluoridation, he could count on reaching his viewers by describing the plan as "a communist plot started by those foreigners in Oak Ridge." And once a mountain blacksmith who took the time to explain to three children that red-hot was not the hottest fire, who awed us by carefully bringing the tip of a white-hot poker close to our noses, told us that we were what his people called "fotched up"—the mountain phrase for *outsiders*.

If the zealous scientific methods and modernist tastes of our community distanced us from the old Tennessee cultures, they did not shield us from the slow effects of the land itself, the hills and high mountains that hold the most flowery forest in North America: redbuds, dogwoods, sourwoods, and tulip trees all blooming over a prolonged spring. With thick mosses, a capillary lace of streams, and snakes shedding papery skins, the forest of east Tennessee gave any wandering child a regard that seemed to preexist even that of her human family. But in those early, postwar years, the living rooms, patios, and lawns of Atom City itself, though immensely historic, were too new to *hold* any history, any layers of time or conservatory custom. In that liminal atmosphere I had the sense that we had all risen up out of the ground overnight, like mushrooms after hard rain. And in fact I suppose we had.

46

\\\\   \\\\   \\\\

Perhaps I especially loved to get in my father's blue car and endure sitting with my two brothers in the back seat for nine hours because we were traveling into deep memory. When our car arrived on the Callahan land in Tuscaloosa County, we walked with great-uncles who spoke familially to paw-paw trees and animals. We walked a red field where my great-grandmother and grandmother had each planted seeds, my grandmother Frances dropping kernels in a row so straight that her father claimed she was the best corn planter in the county. "Better than any of my *boys*," he boasted. My grandmother was proud of that, and recalled her father's praise into her nineties. In red-clay Alabama we sat in parlors, not living rooms, and listened as our grandmother and her twelve siblings remembered. Their mother: Nancy Augusta Speed, a redhead and writer of romantic fiction, a mother then undergoing the Final Stages of Beatification. Their father: the tall newspaper editor "of strong opinions strongly held," who when his lungs sickened from printer's ink, sold his beloved *Eutaw Mirror* and took up farming—"Learned most of it from farm journals and books," said his youngest boy, then newly elected to the state legislature.

On the Callahan porches and in the Callahan parlors, the basic building block of the universe had long ago been discovered and named: it was Talk, and its constituent elements were Mama and Papa, yellow-dog Democrats, grits and red-eye gravy, and, of course, God A-mighty, who was before all building blocks and all universes, and did not approve of gambling—a point on which Albert ("God-does-not-throw-dice") Einstein and the Callahans of Tuscaloosa saw eye-to-eye.

The Callahans were not an insular people; they all set out into the large world, but when they gathered together they liked to remind themselves who they were. When a very large family enjoys its saga—when segments are told and retold, with disputes over crucial details and with laughter rippling a circle of men and women—a listening child might get the idea that *here* is the center of the world. In Alabama, I often felt like a small boat on the sea of their beautiful sounds—Scots-Irish and African cadences met in the Southern new world—and I assumed those sounds were as constant as the sea.

The automobile route from Atom City to the center of the world ran south-southwest alongside the Tennessee River, taking Highway 27 through Spring City and Dayton (site of the Scopes Trial, which our mother, a fan of evolution, reviewed for us), then through Soddy-Daisy (Soddy-Daisy!!) and the gap at Lookout Mountain. From the Cumberland Plateau, we descended into miles of poison-dusted cotton fields, where my younger brothers and I were watchful for the Burma Shave signs then dotted along Highway 11. Whenever a series appeared we sprang into action, chanting the verses. A few of them dealt with the good things that will happen only to a smoothly shaven man ("It gave / McDonald / That needed charm / Hello Hollywood / Good-bye farm"), but the Burma Shave poets were primarily concerned with two great themes, getting the girl and staying alive on the road:

> A beard
> That's rough
> And overgrown
> Is better than
> A chaperone
> —*Burma Shave*

Angels
Who guard you
When you drive
Usually retire
At 65
— *Burma Shave*

We thrilled to those fractured couplets, to the lame verse itself, I'm afraid, and also to the sheer idea of fitting rhymes to the speed and scale of the highway. We felt the American cleverness in those red-and-white signs, were proud to be part of such a country—a witty country, with its poetry inked along the road. *Are we there yet?* Gondolas of coal, and cabooses flew by our windows, and my mother remembers a carful of children who pleaded with their father to stop at every alligator game park, Indian wigwam motel, and fireworks stand along the road. It must have been a nearly continuous pleading, for if the 1950s highways were slow, they did not lack for that sort of wonder.

Lunch was always at a roadside restaurant called Ruby's Chicken-in-a-Basket. No sooner were we settled in our booth than my father would spread his Texaco road map over the table. Was my mother impatient with him for reading the map during lunch, for tracing again the well-known route, and during a meal which even on the road she felt should have a certain tone? I do not remember, exactly, what she said. I only recall my father's determined reply: "I need to know where I am, Dear." And then his hand, deliberately tracing the red and blue lines, a tangle so like the circulatory system. His children, of course, were one of the unmarked reaches, as unlined as the long peninsulas that grew into the gulf.

For as long as I have known him, my father has liked maps, and I have liked to look at them with him—beginning at that roadside lunch stop—hoping to puzzle out a connection between the clear lines marking our location and Ruby's itself, a place where the food came in red plastic baskets. Why didn't they just give us our lunch on plates? was one of my questions. And if it was going to be a basket, why not either use a real straw basket or make the plastic into something that wasn't pretending to be something else, something all its own? And there was the question of our father's intense concern with location and safety, his cautiousness which seemed so tedious to his smooth children.

\|\|\|\| \|\|\|\| \|\|\|\|

When we were young he spoke only rarely about his war, and then always in fragments, whose bone-clean form I have come to admire. Normandy. After the landing at Utah Red Beach. At a fork in the road, and my father's infantry unit is moving into the interior. He is driving ahead to set up communications lines with several other men. A small convoy, my father in the last jeep. He and his pals—he loves these men—reviewed the map earlier, agreed to go right at this fork. It's important. But the lead man makes a mistake, turns left, and the second jeep follows. My father tells his driver to stop, urgently signals his pals by walkie-talkie, waits at the fork for them to return. And then, out of sight, gunfire. "An ambush," the brief story ended.

Unlike the stories in Alabama, our father's short short story was not meant to make anyone laugh, or remember fondly, and there was no satisfied ending such as "And so they did dig that well, and Mama and Papa used that water all their long lives."

In 1954 in the Chicken-in-a-Basket on Highway 11, I did not yet understand my father's wish to examine the map again, to review each detail. Later I would begin to know how war steals some things from people, and gives them other things. And now I might say that my father's scrutinizing of maps, his touching them, folding them up and tucking them in the sun visor, his getting them down and looking at them again was less a way to gauge a route, a route that he knew by heart, than it was a way to review the mystery of survival, to touch its creases as though touching an amulet.

\\\\ \\\\ \\\\

After lunch, our father would fold up his map and tuck it in the felt visor until we pulled into the filling station on the outskirts of Birmingham. *Are we there yet?* We had arrived when we saw the Moon Winx Motel sign—a heart-stopping piece of American road art, a double-sided neon extravaganza; a big taxicab-yellow crescent with a man-in-the-moon on each side, a sly smile, a blue eye that winked, and that blatant misspelling, that X that made us so happy. Two miles beyond the winking moon, the Chrysler's tires would crunch the bed of river pebbles on the Callahan drive. In morning light the pebbles were salmon, ochre, a calcium white— and the water-worn stones, from the one-time bed of the Tombigbee River, closed around our bare feet like cool pockets.

And yet this place was the very place that my mother had left at twenty, feeling surely some of the diffuse stifle that any young person may feel in any enmeshed society—and also wondering, she says, "what kind of life I could have there, because I didn't agree with the treatment of blacks and women." After graduate school in cold Chicago, my mother wrote for the immortal "Which Twin Has the Toni" campaign, listened to jazz, said yes to my father at Wrigley Field, made curtains out of parachutes. Although she has often called me to say "Let's go home," although the accent and manners of her first home are suffused in her every gesture, my mother has little tristesse for a lost place or past. She is the possessor of a mind so open and generally with-it that I have been lulled occasionally into thinking her my complete contemporary, have shocked her by some effluvia beneath the more dignified norms of her generation. (I once asked her the riddle "Do you know why Southern women don't like group sex?"—answer: "Too many thank you notes"—and she was not amused.)

Neither my mother nor my father could afford to look back. It was their child, saturated from infancy in an atomized world, who was tempted to gaze at the vanishing old, and later to bumble in certain vacated shadows. Taking the techno-futurism of my hometown as the norm, I was riveted by the familial rooms of the rural South, its kerosene globe lamps, the dark wood cabinets of radios, shelves of yellowed sewing patterns, the intricate kinship system, the "Damn, brother, I don't believe I'd a-told that!" And also by the knowledge that I belonged, simply by virtue of being the daughter of the daughter of Frances Webb Callahan Watkins. But try as I might, I—who had touched the silver Van de Graaff generator—could never enter into the world of buggies and circuit preachers, and by eight or nine I had also begun to notice that there *were* no mules on their lands anymore, and no circuit preachers riding. My elders were conjuring, with words. Meanwhile, in Oak Ridge, Arthur Snell and I were building a rocketship, for which we had most of the parts we needed.

As my mother and father leaned bravely into the post-war decade, it was easy to feel us all going faster, like the agitated electrons in the museum movie, "preparing," the narrator said, "to jump into another orbit." There was little doubt that we *would* jump, even if we had only a tendency to exist, were ourselves that transparency dancing its radical old jitterbug.

ARTESIAN

|||| |||| |||| |||| ||||

We used water that came fresh out of the overflowing well.
That water was Artesian water—had a touch of mineral in
it. What everybody loved to do was come with a pail to catch
some of that water.

—Frances Webb Callahan Watkins

THE EARLIEST, most primitive earth creatures, the
ones who successfully left the ocean for land, each found some
way to retain a bit of the sea's protean chemistry within the new
land body—water-retaining leaves, blood, a circulatory system,
monthly cycles. Anyone who has ever wanted to retain some of the
salt and life-giving properties of a previous place will admire the in-
genuity of those simple life forms. Their basic situation is now a
commonplace in the diaspora of modernity. In my twenties, settling into New England and with no time to evolve an additional
body part, my water-retaining leaf was made by the Sony Corpora-
tion, and I was often going to Alabama with a tape recorder on my
knee.

"Tape recorder" doesn't scan. We want "banjo." We want the al-
literation of "bama" and "banjo," the little rhyme go and jo, the
suite of a's and b's, and the syncopated iambics of "I've come from
Alabama with a banjo on my knee." A tape recorder could never
generate that, of course, but, O Susanna, technology might hold a

little of the Southern sea, one inlet in particular; might convey to my new home certain sounds that seemed never to be uttered in any part of New England.

For instance, when asked "How are you today?" no one in my chosen city ever replied, as my great-uncle Temo always does, "Mean as a snake." Or, alternatively, "Better than anyone else I know in my condition." And no one in the Boston Basin would say, " 'Course Mama was overjoyed at the news. Her mother was living then. And so Papa carried Mama and the children to Bolingee, and they took Christmas together, were reunited, and everything was right between them ever after."

Consider the phrases "they took Christmas" and "carried Mama and the children." To take Christmas is a slightly different activity than having, spending, or celebrating it. Taking Christmas is a degree more formal, with the hint of taking medicine, communion, or the veil, and also suggesting the latency in the season, a preexistent plenty waiting to be gathered. And how infinitely kind, how nearly transcendentally tender it is to be carried somewhere— to the post office, say—rather than to merely go, drive, or be dropped off there. When we carry a friend to the grocery store, when a neighbor carries us to the station, we are lifting one another, unburdening each other, for a spell, of the burden of ourselves.

These were the everyday sounds of one family, which I had begun to hear at five weeks old, on the August day I was held on Aunt Sister's porch by Wick Watkins. He was then eighty-five, had taken a bus from Bethany and walked another three miles down the road past the water tower to hold his first great-grandchild. He stayed two hours, held the baby, drank a tea (the "iced" in "iced tea" is silent in the South), then walked back to the highway three miles and caught the bus home. I would spend many more hours on that painted cement porch, countless hours playing Go Fish with my grandmother, she managing the dumb wedge of cards while I was mesmerized by the distinctions between diamonds and hearts and never wondering, as I do now, how any adult can love a child enough to play a game like Go Fish for hours.

\\\\\   \\\\\   \\\\\

On those several flights from Boston to Alabama, I was in a hurry. Time was pressing for the generation that had held me in its wiry or soft arms—the soft ones with fleshy upper mounds that I now do everything possible to avoid having, but which were once bliss incarnate. I flew Delta to Atlanta, and changed in Atlanta to one of the tiny prop planes that fly into regional airports. The tape recorder rested in a canvas bag on my lap.

The little plane never flew very high, and as it whined into west Alabama the orange-red soil of the region began to peep between rows of soybeans and sweet potatoes, and to glow on the river bluffs where the earth is forever eroding in rills. The land there is made of yellowish sandy clays, brown loams, and subsoils of purplish-gray. Seen in cross-section on the sides of eroded hills, the colors ripple together, as though a streaming river has momentarily solidified. Descending, the prop plane might pass a plume of sulfurish smoke from the paper mill.

An uncle or cousin would meet me at the airport and drive me through a landscape of planted fields, modern schools, thirties bungalows, and new ranch houses. We passed wash-lines hung with quilts, cola machines snugged to the shank-ends of brick motels, and for a while the road would parallel the Black Warrior River, the wide, slow tributary that joins the Tombigbee at Demopolis. The land through which we were passing first belonged, if land ever does, to the Creek and Choctaw of the Muskogee Alliance. It lies east of the Mississippi border and slightly north of Alabama's Black Belt, the crescent of dark, alluvial soil deposited across the lower part of the state. The region straddles a fault line — a junction in the earth where the soft rock of a coastal plain meets the substrate of a mountain plateau. This fault line marks the southernmost edge of the Appalachias, and passes almost exactly through the land where my mother's people have lived, grown okra, preached, won and lost elections, taught school, said "mash the doorbell" and "cut on the lights," have lawyered, barbered, tended the post office, baked biscuits, and deep-fat-fried more things than you might care to imagine, for more than a century.

Nearing the Callahan acres, we drove past the shack where Wiley Keene lived with his goats, and past the woods through which Hurricane Creek runs along the base of a valley due east of the Callahan land. We passed our late Aunt Sister's land, which begins at a gully along the road and rolls back two hundred yards into a wood. Much of her land is under kudzu now, *Radix puerariae*, the hardy, big-leafed vine which can grow a foot a day, resisting machetes, chemicals, and fire. In places, no branch or leaf of the underlying trees can be seen, only the vines dripping over oaks and sassafras and nondescript thickets like a green icing over the undulations of the earth. The softened, surreal landscape is like none other, remindful only of the Kingdom of Didd, the Seussian land covered when *oobleck* fell from the sky for days.

For several decades after kudzu came, men of our family went out each week to hack the new tendrils, to keep the vines from spreading. At some point their effort failed; the vines leapt the gully and draped themselves across Aunt Sister's property and stole into the forest. As we got out of the car one day, my great-uncle Artemas Killian Callahan, known as Temo, gazed out over the swallowed landscape and said, "It *took* the gully." His voice was warm with admiration, and I realized that this kudzu, generally described as a menace and blight, has become for my uncle, over a lifetime of living with it, a natural, praiseworthy fact. "It cuts down the wash," he said, meaning that it stops the red land from eroding in rain. "Look," he said softly, wading into the *Radix*, and holding up a segment of vine: "Look at what pretty little purple flowers it has." Modestly, under its gulping leaves, the plant grows tiny, orchid-like blooms.

\\\\ \\\\ \\\\

All the tapes I made were recorded in my grandmother's parlor, or the parlors of one of her three living sisters, Mary, Clara, and Nan Dean. The oldest, Sister Faith, had already died at that time; Sam was dead, so were Will, Albert, and James. There are twenty tapes in all, and technically they are rough, with stops and starts, hisses, things being bumped, sudden cries—"Hold it a sec, Aunt Clara, let me get that," as an old lady rises from the couch, catches a microphone cable around her leg, begins to drag the assembly off the coffee table. Once the tape captures a massive thud, and although my ears (our selective wonders) did not notice an outdoor sound at the time, the recorder heard tractor-trailer trucks roaring and whooshing by on the road: as the women are talking, recalling how they cooked a hen chicken in a mud oven, the roar of mobility swells and recedes in the background.

On the tapes, my elders' voices are textured, slow, and smooth, and my voice is higher and faster than it is now. I ask about a wedding souvenir in a scrapbook, about the photograph of two skinny girls in puckered, one-piece suits, posing on sand ("Why, that's your Mama and Mary Grace at Gulf Shores!"); about the sepia portrait of the "outlaws," the men and women who had married into a big family; about the blurry snapshot of two men standing in formal dress by a foothill of peanuts. Some of my questions do launch their tales, including the one about the wanted man that ends with the man apprehended but claiming, as he points to himself, "You've got the wrong man. This here's my brother!" But listening to the recordings twenty years later, I hear myself trying sometimes to steer my relatives to talk about one thing when they wanted to talk about another. Nor was I always attuned to the sudden turns and subterranean channels of an old memory, which could lead Aunt Mary to declare, as we are talking about a Kodak camera, "We wore brassieres. Yes, we did." Or later, while Mary is talking about a child who died young, could move Frances to call out indignantly, "That Kodak camera was stolen at the Birmingham depot, with all my clothes. Never saw it again!"

My idea had been simple. I would a create a slide show, a media form now almost quaint, but cutting-edge in the 1970s, before videos and CD-ROMs. I had already taken hundreds of 35mm slides of photographs from family albums, using a close-up macro lens that copied the whole picture, and also details—eyes and hands, hats and shoes, plows, doors, and spokes of wheels. I imagined that if my relatives would sit around in a group and look at the slides, and use them as points of departure for storytelling, we could create an audio-visual narrative. So I was often trying to get my relatives to tell stories in a way that would synchronize well with the slides (a style that I had learned, probably, from watching documentaries on public television). But the plan often evoked not whole and clear narratives, but comments like "Yes" or "No," "Who took this picture?" "I can't see what it says on this, does it say 'stove polish'?"

There is one whole ninety-minute tape of my relatives watching the slides in their sister Nan Dean's front room. The projector fan whirrs and the slides clank into their slots while voices say:

"That's Mary."

"That's little Cherry."

"That's Arthur."

"No, that's not Arthur,"

"Yes, that *is* Arthur. I'll bet you it is."

"Who's that with Foster?"

"That's not my father. I'd know his face anywhere."

"Well, there *are* things you *don't* know; that *is* Foster, with Ida Mae."

The projected, luminous images of my relative's faces, their houses and wedding gowns, had the effect of turning these great storytellers into spectators, muting their oral tradition. And so the taping sessions worked best when I put the slides away, sat side-by-side with someone on a couch, a photo album on our laps. Most often, my great-aunts merely glanced at a picture to determine its basic situation, then spun into the elastic space-time continuum of a people of the word.

They made a few jokes about the grey box with its buttons and lights, and once my pious, allusive grandmother raised the matter of graven images, saying, "Anyone who would talk into that thing, it would like to be worshipping an Idol." And then she and her sisters ignored the device. They had enough sense of themselves as performers to rise above such a tool in their midst, though they felt its implications: how it made visible something formerly transparent; how it conceded that a culture would not live on in me perfectly. And, too, my project implied Mortality, always a delicate point to imply.

I didn't think that I could hold my old people. The recordings were analog signals, a thin magnetic bridge from memory to memory, meant to trick time a little. They did that, and simultaneously inscribed the very distance that I wished to overcome.

Years later I hear some other things on the tapes that I didn't hear when they were first recorded. During the last five years of her life, my grandmother's memory began to diminish precipitously, and on one of the recordings her sister Nan Dean can be heard becoming increasingly annoyed as my grandmother gropes through a well-worn story about the time the two of them made chicken salad from Uncle Arthur's Dominick hens. "Frances, honey," Nan Dean says finally, angrily, "tell the story right." When there is silence, Nan Dean tells the story herself. I can be heard in the background cajoling the women to speak just one at a time, and trying to bolster my then less brave and articulate grandmother. At the time, I thought that Nan Dean was being bossy and insensitive, but now I hear in her voice that she is terribly frightened, and furious, as her lifelong companion is beginning to slip away.

In her prime, my grandmother told the incident of the chicken salad sandwiches like this:

"Well, your Uncle Arthur just loved chickens, and he had some in the back yard—had a great big old rooster, and some big Dominick hens—*just had chickens*. But Arthur petted everything, and those chickens had become his pets. So he was fixing to do away with raising chickens altogether. The two old Dominick hens were the last ones, they were just hanging on. At that time, Martha Faith, Doris's daughter, was getting married, and Doris was having a reception, going to serve chicken salad sandwiches and ham sandwiches. So Arthur says, 'Well, if she's going to have chicken salad, I'll give those two hens for the wedding sandwiches.' That was the finest thing he could think of to do with his chickens. All right. That took place. So Nan Dean and I plucked and worked and we had a big pan full of the best-looking chicken salad you'd ever want to see in your life. We were stirring it in Nan Dean's kitchen, and I said, 'Nan Dean, I will make a bet with you.'

"'What?' she said.

"'I will bet you a nickel that Arthur Blackman will never take one bite of this chicken no matter what you do to it.'

"'Okay,' she said. 'We'll see.' So she took my bet.

"'All right,' I said. 'I will pass the ham sandwiches for Doris, and you pass the chicken salad sandwiches, and we'll see if your husband takes one.'

"We did all that. And when the time came, Nan Dean passed the chicken salad sandwiches, and Arthur said, 'No, thank you.' That man took a ham sandwich. So Nan Dean had to pay me the nickel. Arthur Blackman would not eat his pet, and he never had chickens anymore."

|||| |||| ||||

These many years later they are all gone but one, the youngest, now ninety-three and without any doubt better than anyone else in his condition. ("You're fiddling in high cotton," he told me recently when I called him from the nation's capital.) Listening to their voices sounding in my New England rooms, I seem to be transported to their kitchens, to their scratchy couches and silk settees. I seem to smell the simmering pots of greens on their stoves, the lemon oil that my grandmother used on her furniture. How can it be that a disembodied, scratchy sound — with nothing of physical form and nothing visual — can bring them so greatly to life in these far rooms? Is it because I knew them first as voices? Occasionally I doze off while listening to their taped voices, much as I did as a girl in one of their parlors, and when I wake up a great-aunt may be, as she was then, in mid-sentence, although sometimes, of course, the tape will have reached the end of its length, and the machine will have clicked off.

What I hear now on the recordings are not so much the facts of their narratives, which are the ordinary facts of our lives — met your grandfather, tended the post office, nuts and oranges in our Christmas stockings, Papa very particular about his shirt-collars — but how they talk, how life's watersheds and minutae are phrased. My grandmother was once speaking about her mother, Nancy Speed, and my mother remarked, "She sounds like a good mother." "Ooouuuweee, there was none better," replied my grandmother, the sound beginning like a factory whistle, drawn out into a little song, then settling into the final emphatic statement: "What she put up with, and how she reared all thirteen of us, is still a mystery to me and I'm *old*."

⦚⦚⦚ ⦚⦚⦚ ⦚⦚⦚

Miraculously the tapes did not get lost, or damaged from leaking oil-paint tubes during the twenty years that they sat in an open cardboard shoebox among miscellaneous art supplies. During those years I moved six times, built closets, put things in the basement, had yard sales. The tapes traveled from place to place undisturbed, the magnetic material growing more fragile over time but suffering no other harm. When at last it occurred to me to transcribe the tapes, and when still later life gave me time to undertake the slow labor, an audio engineer counseled me to duplicate the originals, store the masters in a safety deposit box, and work with copies to avoid straining the old tapes. No sooner were the originals sheltered in a vault behind steel-and-chrome doors than I felt the world, perilous place, had grown slightly safer. (The mind may recognize these efforts as a child's play-dam in the torrent, but seems nevertheless happy and grateful to be fooled.)

Tape transcription is a tedious task and there are many bureaus that perform it here in our university-rich town, but I could not ask another person to tackle these recordings. Few, if any, ears in New England would understand the accents, and no one would care enough to listen again and again to a garbled patch as it slowly clarified. I was glad to do it, and only very infrequently would I give up on a single phrase as irrelevant or too unclear to retrieve. After a while I realized that I was treating the transcriptions as sacred texts, as the shards on which whole belief systems have rested. Gradually, I saw too that the fragments were powerful not only for what they tell, but for what they conceal. The stories my relatives chose to tell after dinner, and also on my recordings, were tales of fecundity and mischief—an account they had worked together over many years like one of their prized quilts. The whole truth came more privately: two women at a kitchen table, an older man talking to a young man by a truck. In those less public places, they spoke of the woman who longed to live among her own people; and of a slow, heartbreaking death, how she could press your hand once for yes, twice for no.

Several of the recorded conversations are less stories than collections of sheerly practical tips; for instance, how to make sorghum syrup from cane, a seminar that began when my mother chanced to ask her mother if she remembered making syrup.

"Oh, yes, sweetheart," my grandmother replies. "Weren't you here when Papa made syrup?"

"Yes, I believe he used a mule," my mother says.

"Yes, and he went 'round and 'round his pole, and the pole turned the wheel that turned the grinder."

"Mama," my mother says, "Mary Grace said Grandpa never had a mule go 'round because he thought that was cruel to the mule."

"Well, he did have a mule!" my grandmother declares. She considers, and adds, "Finally, he had a motor."

"That was always in September, wasn't it, when the cane was ripened?" my mother inquires.

"Well, we had two different kinds of cane," her mother explains, beginning to see that the subject will require clarification. "We had the sorghum, that came first, and then later, in November or late October, we cut the ribbon cane."

"How was the syrup actually made?" I ask.

You can hear the intake of breath as my grandmother is stunned by this ignorance. She cocks her head, visualizing the operation. "All right," she says finally. "There's a long pan that the juice goes in—do you see that?—and there's a furnace goes with it, and that furnace has to be fired with wood. And that boils the sorghum, and as it gets boiling, it goes on, it goes on, it pushes on down a little, pushes on down a little further, and when it's ready, why, they drain it off. And then, of course, you have to have somebody who understands syrup-making. Papa was good at it."

"How did the cane become syrup?" my mother asks, and I nod,

to show that I want to know too. Here Nan Dean interjects, troubled by my mother's question and by my bright face, which show her that although we have just heard the whole operation explained perfectly we are not getting the picture. She is worried for us and for our chances in life, and she begins to speak to us very firmly, in the present tense.

"Now listen. First, you have to cut the cane from growing in the field. Go out into the field, and get the cane. Alright. You've done that. Strip it of its fodder—its leaf—and stack it, right there where you're going to get it. And pick up a stalk and feed it into that grinder. And it grinds the stalks, and your juice comes out of the stalks, and the cane part goes on through just like a flat something, all the juice is flattened out of it. And the pile of that old debris, the old cane, is hauled away, and when it dries you can burn it. And see, all the juice stays in the pan, as she said."

"And it is sweet!" chimes in my grandmother.

"And it's strained!" says Nan Dean. "There's a strainer, so that no sediment would be in the syrup."

"Why do you heat it?" my mother asks, bravely.

"You heat it to cook it, child!"

My grandmother, more patient, tries once more with her only offspring: "See, precious, the PAN is over the FURNACE. IT'S AN OUTFIT!" she says loudly, as though speaking to a hard-of-hearing person. "You have to have the WHOLE OUTFIT to do syrup."

"UNDERSTAND," Aunt Nan Dean suddenly commands, willing us to grasp the process, employing the power that changed the landscape of her county. "UNDERSTAND. You grind the juice, and it falls in that pan, and your grinder sits up there, and the juice falls down in the pan. The pan sits on a little square thing"—she holds up her arms to show its size—"and the pan fits over it . . ."

"Oh no, it's long, Sister. It's longer than that, Nan Dean."

\\\ \\\ \\\

When I first glanced over my shoulder and saw the Past stretching like a prairie as far as the eye could see, I was amazed to discover that such a territory existed, growing all the while, suddenly visible, a tempting place and a frightening one—for who does not feel it ceaselessly gaining, eating away at our little allotment? And as the past reveals itself alluringly to middle-age, one also feels how easily memory conspires with the inventrix nostalgia. Listening to the past could be an escape from the present. Listening to the past could be the flypaper trap for which Dickens gave us the cautionary tale of Miss Havisham and her mouldering cake. And yet, as James Baldwin said, history does not refer merely or even principally to the past, for we carry it inside ourselves, where it whispers to us and shapes the present moment.

\\\ \\\ \\\

"Yes, that's right. It's big!" Nan Dean says, agreeing with her sister. "And you had to watch it to keep from it burning or scorching. It just cooks, exactly like you'd put a thing in a pot on a stove and cook it."

"And as it goes on down and goes on down toward the end, it gets thicker and thicker. You don't want it to get too thick. You have to push it back and push it forward," says my grandmother. "We knew how to do that."

H O S E

⫻⫻⫻   ⫻⫻⫻   ⫻⫻⫻

THE FATTEST WOMAN in the world, circa 1953, lived on Gordon Road in our town. She had a daughter named Alice, who was nine, three years older than me, and one day I asked Alice why her mother was so fat. "She is *not* fat," Alice replied indignantly. "She's pregnant." I could tell from Alice's tone that this was an explanation, but it was the first time the word "pregnant" had been used in my presence and it failed to signify—a triumph that was the product of a long tradition of people saying "in a family way," or "far along," or simply not mentioning it.

Alice and her family, about whom I have no further memory, lived next door to Mrs. Bayliss, an elderly lady whose house sat on the crest of a hill and at the extreme edge of what my brothers and I considered known territory. We had the impression that Mrs. Bayliss lived on a cliff, but looked at strictly topographically in later years, the land only sloped rather gently at Mrs. Bayliss's yard, descending into a thicket of persimmon trees. In late summer the grove exuded a clean, sweet pungency that grew stronger still in fall, after the persimmon fruits had fallen and begun to rot, matting the slope in a slick of overripe pulp and skins.

68

Our house stood on flat, sunny ground, about nine houses away from Mrs. Bayliss and the cliff. One very hot August afternoon, as Kevin Hennessey and I were playing with the garden hose in my front yard, Mrs. Bayliss appeared, walking along the low privet hedge that divided our yard from the sidewalk. She was wearing a silk print dress and close-fitting hat. She wore gloves and carried a patent leather purse over a crooked arm, as the Queen of England did. This was Mrs. Bayliss's marketing outfit, which she wore whenever she walked the half-mile to the A & P grocery in Jackson Square.

I had the garden hose in my hand as Mrs. Bayliss passed in front of our yard, and when the thought came into my mind to point the hose at Mrs. Bayliss and soak her, nothing *intervened*. I did know that it was considered wicked to squirt a jet of water at a grownup, most especially a frail old widow, but something strong overrode this feeble teaching. The sensation of abandoned, transcendent joy that came to me—as the water arched toward Mrs. Bayliss and landed in a great whoosh directly in the middle of her middle—was unparalleled. I had willfully crossed a line and known the ecstasy of dissolving an absolute rule—in this case, decency.

By great good fortune, silk turns very dark when it is wet, and Mrs. Bayliss not only was wet, she looked wet.

For a moment, all three of us stood frozen, staring at one another, unsure if we actually believed what had happened. Mrs. Bayliss's dress was sopping wet and water ran down her face and plopped onto her black patent purse. She must have said something to us at this juncture, but I cannot remember any words, only watching her come slowly to her senses, turn herself around, and go home. Kevin and I played now in the yard in the same frame of mind that bank robbers experience must have after they have pulled off the heist and are back safely in the compound, running their hands excitedly through piles of gold but listening anxiously to the radio for police reports.

In about twenty minutes Mrs. Bayliss reappeared, again walking along the low trimmed hedge in front of our house. She had put on a fresh silk dress and the same hat, had dried off her purse and face. I squirted her again, same as before. The inward, guiding voice had spoken afresh, suggesting that once over the line you might as well linger there a while. I remember that Mrs. Bayliss did speak to us this time—in sharp, high, and memorable if not fathomable sounds. Then she turned around, went home, changed her clothes, came back a third time in a different silk dress, and—*Yes!*

Three times she appeared before us, trusting in our basic goodness; three times she tempted us, and three times we soaked her to the skin. Times two and three, Kevin and I fought over who would do it. But it had been my brilliant idea, and when the blade came down, Kevin was the one who had been "led on" and I was the ghastly child. The fourth time that she set out for the grocery, Mrs. Bayliss turned left at the fork in Gordon Road, rather than right towards our yard (where we waited, poised), and went the long way down Georgia Avenue to Jackson Square to shop.

She called my mother the next day. After replacing the receiver in its cradle, my mother used my full name and told me to come into her room. Language is greatly a tonal affair, and no one could have failed to tremble at the eschatological timbre now flowing in my mother's voice. She said that I should sit down on the ottoman by the window—a round thing with only a rare functionality. During the "very serious talk, young lady" that ensued, my mother's own sunny nature was replaced by the scorches of Presbyterian Hell. Afterwards my mother helped me into one of my fancy outfits, a dress sewn by my grandmother, with dozens of dainty buttons down the front. We practiced my apology several times, and then my mother walked me up the road to Mrs. Bayliss's house on the edge of the cliff, and knocked on the door.

Mrs. Bayliss had always been kind, in a syrupy way, to all the children in the neighborhood, including me. Now, as we waited at the door, I felt not precisely remorse (the feeling my mother had done her level best to arouse) but rather a dim sense that Nature had chosen me to redress this goo of kindness. But this was far too subtle and dangerous an idea of Justice to explore in the moment. I only hung my head in Mrs. Bayliss's house, offered my whispered apology, and then sat in her living room and ate butter cookies. Mrs. Bayliss forgave me and continued being sugary and frail. The only lesson that I learned at the time, if you can call it a lesson, was that for an exquisite joy, for the ineffable feeling of surety, of being perfectly in tune with nature and the gods, there will be a price to pay, and it will be worth it.

Recently I asked my mother, now seventy-five, about this long-ago event and what her point of view was at the time. "My point of view," she replied, the incident coming rather easily to mind, "was the point of view of a mother who wants to crawl under the foundation of the house and never show her face again." My mother also claims that Mrs. Bayliss was neither old nor frail at the time of her soaking. In fact she was not much older than my mother herself, which would have put Mrs. Bayliss in her early forties (younger than I am now). Nor was she a widow—there was a Mr. Bayliss! "And," my mother continues, the ripples of corrective memory sweeping her on, "the dress"—she means *dresses*—"could *not* have been silk. In summer, dear, Mrs. Bayliss would have been wearing *voile*."

About these variances: I doubt neither my mother's memory nor her greater apperception of the victim's character. I can only say that the person she describes is simply not the person I squirted, though I grant that the dresses were very likely voile.

The savage glee of that afternoon lodged firmly in mind and body, where it seems to contrast completely with my present moral life. I am often these days trusted not only with hoses but with several hearts, sharp knives, and jumper cables. Recently I traveled from my home in New England to Gordon Road, and the woman who answered the door let me wander a while in a yard where the hemlock planted for my birth has grown taller than her house. I stood under the maple where Kevin and I liked to open wing-like seeds, stick the cases over our noses, walk around like that. Mrs. Bayliss, I was sorry to learn, had died, only the year before. How I would like to have visited her once more, or taken our chances on a walk down the hill to Jackson Square. Could I have found a way to thank her? It would have been a delicate undertaking, involving the risk of appearing completely unreconstructed. But I might have tried, for by her person, by her profoundly misplaced trust, the lady Mrs. Bayliss provided me a singular and pristine happiness, undimmed across four decades.

HYMN

‖‖ ‖‖ ‖‖

"This is going to be one of those things going to grow."
—Maude Thompson,
   in Eudora Welty's "A Pageant of Birds"

THE SCHOOL FOR THE SPIRIT is everywhere and unofficial, but when I was a child an awful lot of the formal spiritual education I was to receive took place in a room in a cinder-block building called the Annex—a consecration of folding chairs, library paste, and construction paper in assorted colors. In that school, we learned the Ten Commandments, and how to be a shepherd in the Christmas pageant. We learned a phrase I have not forgotten—"the still, small voice"—and we learned hymns. Each week, one or two children were asked to select the hymns for our children's service; one week a timid, tow-headed boy sat by my side as we leafed through wafer-thin pages, and I chose "Wasn't That a Mighty Day," "Wade in the Water," and "Go Down, Moses."

The hymn numbers were chalked on the board (you just gave the numbers not the titles, to the teacher), there was a reading, and then we recited the prayer we were learning, being careful and proud to say "Forgive us our debts as we forgive our debtors," in the Presbyterian way, rather than "trespasses" and "those who trespass against us," as my Southern Baptist relatives did—the problematics

73

the two phrasings posed in a child's mind, both individually and in comparison (property lines? bankers?), being a detour of too great a magnitude to entertain here. When it came time to sing, we turned in our hymnals to the numbers on the board. We did the first song and were turning to the second when one of the teachers suddenly halted the proceedings, searched our faces, and asked, "Who chose these hymns?"

The question was not entirely accusatory, nor admiring, nor at all easy to interpret. The timid boy and I must have looked the most miserable of the miserable, for the teacher's eyes came to rest on us. I had not abandoned a slight hope that perhaps we were being singled out for praise, but after it had been determined who had been the active agent, I merely received a Long, Hard Look. Those were the days when a look was still a full player in the house of manners. The teacher herself then selected other hymns (dull ones), and afterwards the morning went on in an ordinary way until we were released to run to our parents in the fellowship hall of the church proper, where we squirmed until they finally stopped socializing and we could race to our family cars, be driven home, take off our fancy clothes, and at last, over my mother's chicken and dumplings and the *Knoxville Sentinel*, return to the regular world. But I was changed.

For the rest of that morning, I hoped by a mimic of normalcy to paper over the gulf that had opened between myself and society. I had chosen bad hymns. Or not bad, exactly, because what would they be doing in the hymnal in the first place if they were not good? Adults often gave you a reason, however tenuous, for their rules: "Look both ways because a car might be coming" or "Eat your flan because your mother made it specially." But in the case of what were then called Negro Spirituals, there was no cause-and-effect formula offered as to why we should not want to sing them. I grasped that the matter, whatever it was, was not theological, was rather a social nuance, and I suspected that it had to do with the spine-tingling quality of my chosen songs—hymns that were stately and high-toned with longing and sorrow, and also, curiously, with far more happiness than could be found in the regular grizzled psalmodies and Lydian measures.

There was a good deal about the situation that a seven-year-old could not grasp. I did not know that during the Civil War the Presbyterian Church had split into Northern and Southern branches, that in nearby Knoxville, Presbyterians had sided with the Union, and that ever since, some of the Presbyterian churches in our region, although geographically Southern, followed the liturgy and policies of the Northern branch. Moreover, most citizens of our town had come from other regions of the country, even other countries, to distill uranium and do atomic research. Oak Ridge was hardly a typical Southern town, and yet when Christine Barnes and I went to McCrory's Five & Dime we passed two water fountains, one of them labeled with a hand-lettered cardboard sign. We had seen the Jim Crow sign as long as we had been coming to the dime store, and we found it not exactly repulsive—we didn't have the consciousness for that—but in some way shabby. We didn't like it and we defied it. Many times when we were eight or nine, Christine and I went to the "colored" water fountain and drank from it. Our act was a combination of scientific interest—calmly testing to see what would happen to ourselves or to the five & dime if this curious division were breached—and a child's inborn antenna for the weak places in adult logic.

Tennessee in the early fifties was a segregated state, although the mountainous, hardscrabble communities of Appalachia had never been conducive to the plantation and share-cropping systems, and many of the black inhabitants of Oak Ridge had migrated from Mississippi to labor in the secret bomb factories. In Oak Ridge during the war years, they discovered one of the most intentionally segregated communities in the country; Manhattan Project officials had carefully set up the town's housing and commercial districts to conform to prevailing racial customs of the region. By the late 1940s, scientists and religious leaders had begun to object. Oak Ridge would send white pastors to Selma with books for black churches, would desegregate its own public places, pools, movie houses, and restaurants more willingly, perhaps, than any other Southern town: a group of white men guaranteed the first white barber to integrate his shop all their business; black and white women created a day-care center and swim programs. But progressive Oak Ridge was layered over the original racist patterns and during the 1950s, African-American citizens lived and went to elementary school apart, in a segregated part of town.

It was in this unusual town, in a border state, in my parents' music cabinet, that I first discovered black gospel: a handful of recordings tucked amongst Charlie Parker's "Bird of Paradise," the operas *Turandot* and *Der Rosenkavalier*, and a single of Rudy Valleé singing "As Time Goes By." For listening to the translucent orange records of "The Little Engine That Could" and the terrifying "Tale of the Grasshopper and the Ants," my younger brothers and I had a small portable record player. But after we were trained in the placement of the needle on the empty band at the beginning of a record, we were allowed to use the adult phonograph—*quietly.* Sitting on the floor with my back resting against the cabinet, I listened over and over to several thick 78s, mostly of Mahalia Jackson (accompanied by Mildred Falls) rendering the slow poetry of "Take My Hand, Precious Lord," and the flattened thirds and sevenths of "If You See My Savior, Tell Him That You Saw Me." These were the compositions of Thomas A. Dorsey—not *Tommy* Dorsey, but the synthesizing genius first known as Georgia Tom, who layered blues tropes over religious hymns, migrated north to the steel mills, and began to create gospel-blues at the Pilgrim Baptist Church of Chicago. A little older, I would listen to the Golden Gate Jubilee Quartet, to Blind Willie Johnson singing his eerie, strangled 1929 recording of "Let Your Light Shine on Me," and to the wall of sound that came from Ira Tucker and the Dixie Hummingbirds.

I was listening, unawares, to recordings made in the wake of the success of the Mills Brothers, gospel songs arranged in jazz, boogie, and blues-influenced styles that appealed to white as well as urban black audiences. It would be many more years before I found the small, independent-label recordings of the more rural gospel tradition, and of the early Depression era choirs, and quartets from the black colleges singing "Get Right, Stay Right" and "I'm In a Strange Land."

Meanwhile, the few records I did know hissed around the felt plate of the record player in our living room—the sound issuing the haunting bent note of the Southern new world. As Mahalia went "sightseeing in Beulah," I sang with her, forgetting that my grandfather, a fine baritone, had declared, "Child, you cannot carry a tune in a *basket*." No matter; Mahalia and I had feasted with the Rose of Sharon, had been on speaking terms with the spirit. It was not only the words, each one a physical fact, each one opened up, entered into and walked around in, but the majestic juice of the sound—the sweeping river of the woman's voice, bigger than any woman in our science town had ever allowed herself to sound, and the going so low, so sweetly, so solidly of the male voices. There was a moan at the center, and even so, long after the record went back into its cardboard sleeve there was gladness and buoyancy. It was a serious sound, and it also jumped. This was more than song. This was philosophy, which children are always on the alert for, as well as for all evidence that adults are pleased to be alive.

To try to say entirely why one loves what one does seems not only a fruitless task, but a little wrongheaded, on the order of dissection and with those consequences. "Who chose these hymns?" The answer, needless to say, was that the music had chosen me, and mercifully I was yet too innocent to wonder whether I had any right to what was on that handful of 78s in my parents' music cabinet. By the time I had grasped the ironies of my rhapsodizing to black gospel, and soon to the Delta blues of Son House and Robert Johnson, the *cri de coeur* of Bessie Smith—by the time I understood that my life offered possibilities whose prolonged absence was one of the provocateurs of African-American lyrics—by that time buses of freedom riders would be rolling south toward Anniston and Birmingham.

But that was still a little in the future. It was a summer in the early fifties, and I was perhaps seven the Sunday afternoon I sat with relatives on a front porch in Alabama and saw a long line of black folks coming along the dusty red shoulder of the road beating tambourines, shouting and singing in a celebration unlike any I had ever witnessed in Atom City. "They've let out at Hurricane Baptist," said my Aunt Clara. "Looks like somebody got saved this morning." I was ready to go to the road—to follow along or be closer, I didn't know—but my aunts said, oh no, that would be tacky, rude, impolite, and not done. (Tacky was, I knew, in a way worse than wickedness, which is rooted in original sin and subject to forgiveness, whereas tackiness is something you ought to be able to avoid altogether.) "You stay right here on the porch," they said.

Most, not all, of my Southern relatives spoke respectfully of their black neighbors, with whom they shared a god, speech patterns, cuisine, Hurricane Creek, and the Alabama heat and wilting humidity. At that time, my grandparents and great-aunts and -uncles were firmly embedded in the culture of segregation, but personally, in that curious, oft-remarked doubleness of the South, they were neighborly. They and their African-American neighbors had lived on adjacent lands for a long time and their connection was real: collard greens, peanuts, tools, and sick-bed courtesies were exchanged. A great-uncle did legal work for his African-American neighbors gratis, mostly routine matters, but once his intervention with the court spared a man named Oscar Prince from an undeserved and hideous fate. Over the course of their lives, many of my relatives traced the logic of their faith through to its radically beautiful conclusions. And yet it was clear enough in the early fifties, sitting on a porch, going to a five & dime, singing in a Sunday school, that there existed some ill-defined but strong line that was not to be crossed.

Most of a century has passed since W. E. B. Du Bois named that line and called it the problem of the twentieth century, but as the millennium arrives the legacy of the color line is still palpable in American life. One of the times that line is still deeply inscribed and observed is Sunday morning. Decades had passed since that hour on a porch in Alabama. I was nearing fifty, and had been living in New England for twenty years the cold winter morning I woke up ready to heed an old intuition.

\|\|\|\| \|\|\|\| \|\|\|\|

The church is located between a U-Haul warehouse and a Shell filling station. On Sundays members may park in the lot of a defunct nightclub across the street. The church building is a late nineteenth-century structure clad in shingles, with a tower that was once struck by lightning. The entrance doors are made of a honey-colored wood and have a bas relief cross on each panel. Inside, a congregation is busy this morning getting children into their small red robes and getting the four choirs of the Combined Choirs combined.

"Merry Christmas and welcome to Union!" calls a woman bustling across the foyer.

The sanctuary is up two flights of stairs, a great room with rows of turned maplewood columns that support a wide mezzanine and organ loft. There is a rainforest of poinsettias on the altar, and set high in the chancel wall, a diamond-shaped stained-glass window, which is refracting a low winter sun into a beam of light. Over the next several hours of the service, the beam will scan slowly across the room, surrounding one person after another in a violet nimbus. There are about four hundred people in the pews. I notice, of course, that three hundred and ninety-nine of us are chestnut or chocolate-brown, or the color of *café au lait*, or of toffee, or blue-black, or an ochre-brown—the great spectrum of hue we improbably collapse into the single word "black"—and that I am the shade the Japanese call pink, that graphic designers specify as PMS 475, a light beige improbably called "white." But I knew this would be so, and I confess that I, lover of hats, am also noticing the hat line. I am one of the few women present not wearing a great hat. Except for weddings, funerals, and brief prayers in tiny, candle-lit chapels on Greek islands, this is my first morning inside a church in three decades. Hat envy is not the first feeling the prodigal wants to have upon her return, but there it is. I could be wearing a great hat *too*, I think—and without one I feel incompletely dressed. A lady nearby wears a ruddy turban with a single saffron plume fixed to the front of the turban by a green pin. The plume is delicate, and it moves in the air gently, like the antenna of a genteel space being. A few rows ahead, there is a sedate-looking deep red hat with a wide brim, the underside of which is solid rhinestone. There is a beret worn by an elderly woman at the perfect Parisian angle. There are African wraps, a Moroccan pillbox, hats with veils, netting, and beads, and a high modernist hat that looks like the upswept roof of Dulles Airport.

A number of years have now passed since that December celebration, and I have had cause to think in that great room about more than hats. Everyone knows that the black church in America is a rock and a beacon, and there are others far more steeped in its ways and history, more qualified to speak of its nature than a white woman who does not rest within any one belief system. But surely anyone of any faith or ancestry may feel the moral fire that has moved in this church and others like it. Anyone may register the *gravitas* of its rooms. Anyone may notice that this church is a place of routine loveliness, an American place where respect for elders, formal address and courtesy titles, the honed artistry—the sheer comeliness of the community—is sanctuary in itself.

∭ ∭ ∭

It is the oldest women, the matriarchs of the church, who are the first to extend a welcome, the first to ask my name, where I live, am I married. These women pat my hand, saying things like

"Bless you, child, come back and see us." It pleases me more than I can say, not only to be so graciously received, but to observe a group of elderly women wielding their power to size someone up. During the earliest months I attend this church, my pew mate is most often Doris Callender. ("Miss," she corrects me when I say Mrs. Callender, "I'm Miss.") Miss Doris Callender is a small woman who often wears a blue felt hat and always sits near a stained-glass window where, without eyeglasses, she follows scripture in a tiny Bible printed in tiny type—a text that is to my younger eyes only a blur.

Many mornings the message for me comes not only from the pulpit but from Miss Callender, who has just turned eighty. I know because her birthday offering of eighty dollars was printed in the bulletin. "One for every year the Lord has given me," she told me. She is reserved but kindly, and one morning discreetly slips me a tissue when she sees me dabbing my eyes. When I thank her, she whispers, "That's what we're here for, to help each other," proposing an answer to life's most pressing question in nine soft words.

I sit next to Miss Callender and another woman, a widow I'll call Gladys Reed, through April and May, and in June of that year a heat wave settles over New England. One sweltering Sunday the sanctuary is aflutter with paper fans donated by a local funeral home—exactly the kind of fans that my great-aunts kept on their front porches and in their parlors, the kind of paper fans printed in over-the-top Maxfield Parish colors and stapled to flat wooden sticks that resemble giant tongue depressors. The sermon is underway and the room is growing warmer. As a young, white-gloved woman—officially, an "Usherette"—passes our pew, Gladys Reed silently pantomimes that she requires a fan. The Usherette whispers apologetically that the fans have run out, whereupon Mrs. Reed silently fixes her with a look. It is swift and momentary, and in another room it might not even be noticed. But here, where elders are treasured—are attended—the younger woman fully absorbs the meaning: an elder wants a fan right this minute. Scurrying, the Usherette returns with an extra program that Mrs. Reed might use in lieu of a fan. My seatmate barely glances at it, dismissing the patently absurd idea of using a program as a fan. Next, the top part of a fan is brought—an old and battered cardboard lacking its wooden handle. Mrs. Reed sniffs, moves her hand in a minimalist gesture. Stricken, the Usherette disappears. Ten, fifteen minutes pass and the room grows warmer. And then the young woman reappears—flushed and out of breath, clearly having *left* the church, driven many blocks to the funeral home, picked up new fans, driven back, raced inside and upstairs to the sanctuary, and hurried down the aisle to present Mrs. Reed with the first from a stack of new, whole fans. This is proper and good. Gladys Reed accepts the fan with the faintest of nods.

\|\|\| \|\|\| \|\|\|

This community of old-fashioned civilities is pastored by the Reverend Jeffrey L. Brown, a lean, brilliant man with a droll sense of humor and what one of his co-pastors calls an "on-fire heart." Not yet forty, Brown is also chairman of the Boston Ten Point Coalition, a group of progressive urban ministers whose effect among our city's most disenfranchised young people has been so profound that the coalition's model is being translated to Tampa, Louisville, Detroit, Philadelphia, and other urban centers. The Ten Point Coalition has caught the eye of government policymakers, who are looking at the possibility that faith-based institutions, specifically the black church, may have the know-how to renew the inner cities. And it has caught the eye of leaders in Bosnia, South Africa, and Rio, other places where children suffer from nihilism rooted in injustice, violence, and poverty. The Reverend Brown studied at Harvard but he learned to preach—we can be thankful—elsewhere, beginning at the foot of some master in a hamlet of North Carolina. Brown is at home penning editorials for the *Boston Globe*, leading a prayer protest in the Rotunda of the U.S. Capitol, delivering a scholarly paper, negotiating a midnight peace with gang members, and visiting a crosstown Unitarian pulpit. In his own pulpit Reverend Brown can, as he puts it, "cut loose."

Across America, more black women than white are in the pulpit, although until recently most of them have ministered to small congregations in storefront and home-based churches. Following traditions that Africans brought to America, women in mainstream African-American churches have considerable authority as worship leaders, prayer warriors, and teachers. Officially, however, the major black Christian denominations have been as slow as their white counterparts to ordain women. It is notable then that at Union Baptist, Jeffrey Brown shares the pulpit with two distinguished women: the Reverend Dr. Cheryl Townsend Gilkes, prominent scholar of African-American studies and sociology of religion; and the Reverend Zina Jacque-Bell, a luminous innovator. About this trio I feel what everyone must, which is the luck we feel when, say, a couple of planets and a full moon make a rare conjunction in the evening sky. Each week the pulpit at Union is alive with story and exegesis of text, with cultural diagnosis and calls to action, with counsel for souls, and flashing wit—all interwoven in the best tradition of black sacred oratory: "God's trombones," James Weldon Johnson named the men and women who inhabit the black pulpit. Lucid and subtle on the significance of Job's suffering, bracing on the nature of courage, passionate on the supreme importance of nurturing children, Reverend Jeffrey Brown usually manages to work into his remarks how fine someone looks—or how fine *everyone* looks — and the fact that Bible study is at 6:30 Wednesday night.

This sanctuary is also a home to the sounds that have spoken to me from the beginning, that inexplicable alchemy of longing and joy. Here, a middle-aged woman in sunglasses sings a bluesy version of "Can't Nobody Do Me Like Jesus" that could qualify as one of the proofs. Here, the congregation stands each week to sing choruses of "Glad to be in the service / glad to be in the service / glad to be in the service one more time" — several hundred people on their feet giving every human indication of gladness. "GOD IS GOOD," an elderly man declares. "ALL THE TIME!" responds a chorus. Here, as a pastor makes an especially nice point, a young man shouts, "TELL THE WORLD!" A woman in a trim business suit stands: "TEACH!" she calls, in a penetrating voice that zings through the air and lands on the pulpit like a flower thrown to an opera star. The woman raises one arm, waves it slowly, back and forth above her head. More ladies stand up and the air is full of graceful waving arms. Four men begin a chorus with the word "Well," making an antiphonal exchange with the preacher — the simple word elongated into two syllables, rising at the end like an encouraging question:

"There is one more thing . . ." the Reverend says.

"Weh — ell?" chant the men in unison.

"The Christmas message came from someone in *particular* . . ."

"Weh — ell?" say the men.

"From someone who could not stay at the *hotel* . . ."

"Weh — ell?"

Here, pastors often begin in a whisper, and slowly, with the sermon as one text and the voices of the congregation another, build voice until the room is a sea of "SAY THAT!" "FIX IT! FIX IT!"

and "PREACH!"—the call-and-response tradition whose template must be the creative play and reciprocity in life itself. On any morning the air is rich in metaphor: living water, the tender hand that lifted me, friend and comforter, redeemer, mighty maker, the lamb, the lily, the love divine. And still, many days the Reverend Brown must stand back at last from the pulpit and shake his head, arrived at the border of silence, the depth of feeling where no words may go.

Among the linguistic traditions are the testimonials given before the official service begins. Every Sunday morning someone will stand up to give thanks because "He woke me up in my right mind this morning!" An octogenarian will rise to say "I'm breathing today, I have a roof over my head, and I'm *satisfied!*"

It is while listening to the clarified voices of one church that I too remember to be glad when I wake up in my right mind, glad for the roof, glad for breath. How simple it is, but it is, of course, *the* shift— the turn, the conversion from a constant whine to the bass note of gratitude. It is not an easy turn for anyone in this culture, which treats all its citizens to the cruel premise that there is no such thing as enough. It could not have been an easy turn for these elders, who have had more reason than most Americans to doubt Providence. What a subtle thing is going on here: at the same time that this community is steadily helping its members gain a fair share of the nation's goods, it is steadily infusing material reality with another idea of wealth altogether.

\\\   \\\   \\\

Like other black churches in America, this one is both an oasis and a center of community life: meals for the homeless, fashion shows, Kwanzaa celebrations, career-day fairs, scholarship awards, tribute dinners, lectures, and the purely social gatherings Union refers to as "having a good time in the Lord." Once upon a time, the membership would have come largely from the immediate city neighborhood, but as many African-American families have migrated to the suburbs, members now return to this church from all points on the metropolitan and socio-economic map.

One morning the theme from the pulpit is inclusion—meant to address the multicultural diversity *within* the black community: the Caribbean, Afro-Latin, Euro-African, and African-American heritages represented in the congregation. Some of the things said: That you cannot be judging one another, for we don't know who is an angel among us, might be an angel come into our midst. That cliques are forming in the church and Reverend Brown does not like that. That the church is not the building, not the pastors, not the officials. The church is not the choirs, great and fine as they are. No, the church is *love*. And another thing—the Reverend does not want to *hear* about anyone not coming to church because of not having the right thing to wear. He recalls being a small boy sent into church to secure a pew for the family, remembers rushing in without his coat, being stopped, being told he could not come into church without a coat: "That brother didn't know if maybe I didn't *own* a coat," Reverend Brown fumes. "I will *never* forget that. Couldn't *come* into the church because I didn't have a coat! As long as I am Pastor," he declares, "anybody can come in here in *anything*. If there is some raggedy person outside wants to come in, I'll go out and bring them in—*personally* set them down."

He means it, and the church describes itself as having "the widest doors in the city." This is a place that aspires to *communitas*, where society's distinctions are softened. So I am also welcomed. All visitors are warmly welcomed. But when it seems that I might be something more than an ephemeral visitor, a great tentativeness comes upon me. The church has long been black America's most precious institution, *the* institution that African Americans completely control, nurturing place of leaders, of artistry and mind—the place where a microcosm of sanity and goodness could be conjured. I can only imagine that many members must cherish one realm free of whites.*

Given history, given the chosen apartness of many blacks in the post–Civil Rights era, what Clarence Page has called the "social apartheid," does my presence diminish the creative refuge of this sanctuary? I don't yet know anyone in the congregation well enough to ask outright, and my smattering of African-American friends are either bemused or appalled to learn that I am going to *any* church. Like me, these friends left organized religion long ago, and are either still getting over it or have taken refuge in the Buddha or in their art, spending many Sundays, as I have, in one of nature's cathedrals, or in what Wallace Stevens memorably called the "complacencies of the peignoir."

The dearest of these friends looks at me earnestly. "You want to know what the members of that church are thinking about you? They're thinking 'Uh oh, there goes the neighborhood!'" He holds his serious face a moment longer, then bursts out laughing. "I couldn't resist," he says. "Actually," he continues, now truly serious, "I have no idea what they're thinking. And you know better than to ask me that." He wags his finger at me. "Why do you assume I'll know what other black folk are thinking? You need to realize that your church is very different from the one I grew up in. We were never hallelujah people, except for my Aunt Ethel. I grew up just

---

*"Of white *control*," Reverend Brown will later write in the margins of this essay.

like you did, in a Presbyterian church. And we were *quiet*, we were God's frozen people. One more thing," Tippy adds firmly. "Don't get any ideas about me coming with you."

Another friend also levels with me. "Don't hope for a welcome from everyone," she says. "But remember, your spiritual life isn't *about* other people's approval." She pauses. "Now, if you don't mind me asking, girl, why are you going?"

\\\\ \\\\ \\\\

My reasons go back very far, but as it happened I began to attend a church named Union during the years when black and white Americans were beginning to say out loud that, for all the gains, we still do not know each other well, do not frequent one another's social worlds, that the line may even be congealing again. In my own life, I have only rarely been in predominantly black gatherings, and almost never just incidentally. In Union's rooms I am doing only a little of what African Americans have done a good deal of for three centuries—sojourning in institutions dominated by another group, adapting, becoming adept in style-switching. But crossing the color line is different, of course, for the historical oppressor than for the historically oppressed, and though I gain a keener sense of how it feels, viscerally, to be radically in the minority and to lack insider knowledge, to assume this status voluntarily, for a few hours each week among people of good will, is hardly a parallel to black America's experience.

Less agile at the crossing than are members of this community, in the beginning I am also hyper-aware, ever mindful to present a positive face of whitedom—a self-conscious, walking-on-eggshells politesse that can make me clumsy. One morning as I stand for a

· responsive reading, the hymnal in my hand grazes the head of an elderly man in the pew in front. Holy moly, I have hit an elderly black man on the head with a hymnal! I lean down to apologize, and as I do, the old gentleman turns his head to look at his wife, possibly thinking it was she who touched his head. He now receives a second shock—an unfamiliar white face looming just inches from his own—and he starts. He visibly jumps in the pew. His startlement startles me, and I jump too, and no one near us fails to see this scene. Most manage to keep a straight face, but the small boy next to me begins to giggle. His mother frowns at her boy and then at me, too, and as soon as possible the boy and I slink down on our pew, silently, side by side, each of us, for our own reasons, trying to contain ourselves.

In another church, I might volunteer for something as a gesture of good intentions, but here I grasp that the most respectful thing to do is to do nothing. Is to wait. (And to try not to hit anyone else with a hymnal.) There is no quick, easy way to override the long accumulation of meaning that America has ascribed to color, and here there will be only personal answers to the matter of my presence, across the usual vagaries of human chemistry. A few members are cool at first, but the great majority are entirely gracious, and several—a retired professor, several of the deaconesses and pastors, and Union's great tenor, Emma Nance—go out of their way to give me clues and actual things to do. One day, after a committee meeting, I am in conversation with a woman who has become overworked at the church. She's going to take a break, she says, to take stock. I applaud her decision, then observe that I am in the opposite situation, that my participation is limited—by history, I say. "Well," Jane replies, "some people do get stuck in the history.

Oh my yes, the history is *there*—but it doesn't have to define us."

James Baldwin was thinking about how to negotiate this history when he predicted that any real dialogue between blacks and whites would require a personal confession from whites that is "a cry for help and healing," and a personal confession from blacks "which fatally contains an accusation." One Sunday not long after I read that passage, Reverend Gilkes is in the pulpit: "I am talking about our men this morning," she says. "Our men can be paid to be entertainers and basketball stars, but the enemy will not open the doors of higher education! The enemy will not let our men become educated! And if one of us gets over, the enemy changes the rules!"

The Reverend catalogues the effects of the enemy's ways—the numbers of black men in prison, the number apt to die before twenty-one—and she likens America's black men to Samson, who, when shorn, blind, and imprisoned could yet summon a divine strength to crumble the house of his captivity. "We will tear *down* the enemy's walls," she says, her voice is blazing now, her arms outstretched. The woman has reached her voice down into the torment of centuries; seems to be speaking for all that time. The other pastors stand and go to her, gather around close, as if to hold and bank her cathartic fire. The wooden floor of Union begins to rumble under a slow stamping of feet, and the whole room is weeping.

Afterwards, as I remain seated, sobered, Dr. Grainger Browning comes up, greets me in his usual ebullient manner, then lingers to ask, "What was that like for you, to hear that sermon, what I'd call a completely black sermon?" He pauses. "I mean," he continues, "it happens to us all the time, to be the only one in a crowd, hearing something from a completely white point of view, but what is it like for you to hear that kind of sermon?"

A former professor of sociology, Dr. Browning is curious, and he is also being kind, guessing that I might feel, as of course I do, a mingling of implication and empathy. I form some words about solidarity, but my friend interrupts. "I know your politics," he says. "You probably agree with the sister more than I do. What I am asking is how did it *feel*, how did it feel to hear a sermon from a completely black point of view?" Before I can muster an answer, Dr. Browning continues. "You know, I don't think in terms of black or white much anymore," he says. "I really don't. Of course I notice. I'm not color-blind; I'm not that far yet. But I do not let it affect my actions. I check myself. And as a teacher, I made sure that I was fair to all my students. I think that there is a percentage of us now, not the majority, but maybe twenty percent of people, both black and white, who will not divide along racial lines, who will not let that happen again to our country—people who are standing in the gap, just wanting to solve it."

|||| |||| ||||

Much of what happens in this great room happens in other rooms where people gather to think about meaning, to give thanks for the blooming universe. But some of what takes place here is unique to the black church tradition. One of the pastors makes an allusion to that uniqueness one day. She is praying: "Lord," she says, "we are the descendants of a people who *chose* to survive. We are *your* people and we have come together this morning to worship you in a special way—for we have a special history, and a special way of knowing you."

The special world inside these walls is not an inversion of the pathology outside its doors—that is, it is not a world of presumed black supremacy. The temptation to imagine such a place must be great, if only as a poetic justice. And certainly African Americans, who have long observed the debasing effect of racism on whites, may know a moral refinement that an oppressor cannot. But something more original than inversion is at work, a move that slips the knot of reaction. There are many veins of African-American spirituality, of course, but among the several Christian forms there are common themes. In today's seminaries, scholars understand black theology as a distinctive interpretation of Christianity. Building on African metaphysics, on a view of the universe as informed by benevolence, black American Christians have drawn especially on the social justice teachings of Amos, Isaiah, Hosea, and Micah, on Christ's love for the neglected, and on the Exodus into a promised land. The symbolic narrative of black Christianity is one of survival and resistance—and creativity. The story is told in a highly allusive language, and language that moves easily between stately and earthy tones, between redemption and fish fries—language that presents the temporal and spiritual as inseparable.

Many have agreed with Dr. King that the African-American saga transcends its historical particulars to speak to common human hopes. For generations the black church has been at the heart of that saga, and Reverend Brown now speaks of his spiritual tradition as a body of thought that offers what he calls "correctives" to dominant culture—a moral and intellectual discourse that issues a steady call for America to fulfill its promise.

We might think that a place that can do that—a place that fueled one of the great transformations of our society, and which has preserved real community through the twentieth century—is a place that has some clues, not only for its core members, but for the larger community of the nation.

\\\\ \\\\ \\\\

Entering slowly into the life of one church, I begin to grasp how many of my hopes for America, and even the style of my generation, can be traced to communities like this one. "Oh yes," says Reverend Gilkes one day in conversation. "Whites have always liberally borrowed elements of black spirituality and style. And white people love our spirituals, our music. But traditionally, they have never accepted black *leadership*."

\\\\ \\\\ \\\\

One morning as we are singing "Walk in the light, walk where the dewdrops of mercy shine bright," my eye happens to land on the mirror above the organ loft. A great swath of the congregation appears in the reflection and among us there is one jarringly pale face. "Who can that be?" I think, and am surprised, seconds later, to realize the answer. The wish to belong, to know and be known, is deep in us. And the wish to travel, to expand into the unknown, to carry messages across borders, is also deep. Both instincts are probably linked with survival, though the traveler is sometimes viewed with wariness. Hermes, ancient god of travelers, is not only a guide but a trickster, very like Eshu Elegbara, the African guardian of the crossroads, another of those changeful figures that show up in every culture.

Old pagan emanations such as Hermes and Eshu are probably not often admitted to the church basements of Christendom, but some kind of shape-shifter hovers there the first time I cook for a church supper. I have made a large pot of Portuguese kale soup, a hearty, fragrant soup that people have loved at my table for twenty years. (You can put a dollop of sour cream on top, if you like.) I am attending my soup from behind the buffet table, a ladle in hand. We are located between a bubbling macaroni-and-cheese casserole and a huge bowl of rice and peas. The first arrivals through the buffet line look at the unfamiliar soup skeptically.

"What is it?" asks one hungry teenage lad.

"Portuguese kale soup," I say, proudly, ladle raised for action.

"I'll have the macaroni casserole, thank you."

Nine or ten more people in line give Portuguese kale soup one look and pass it up. My debut is not going well.

Finally someone comes along who asks, "Is it collard greens?"

"No, it's kale greens."

"No thanks," he replies. But he has given me a clue.

"It's greens and beans," I say, truthfully, to the next person who asks, who is the choir director, Brother Philip.

"Oh, I'll have some," he says. And, upon tasting this greens and beans, adds loudly, "It works for me."

Brother Philip's endorsement gets me two more takers, and then a young lady comes along who peers with interest at the soup.

"This looks like an Italian minestrone," she says hopefully.

"Well, yes," I say. "It's a lot like minestrone—almost exactly."

The young woman has two helpings and her girlfriend asks for the recipe. Hovering near the line, but not in it, is a young man who has obviously overheard the several names already given to this soup. Now he steps up to the buffet table with a sly grin.

"I wonder if your soup could be a jambalaya?"

"Yes," I say without hesitation or shame. "It's jambalaya."

"Oh, this is my lucky day," he says, chuckling. "So, if you will, please put that jambalaya over the rice and peas. Not too much sauce," he adds, showing me how to make the concoction. Tasting the melange, he says, "That's *bug!*"

Now all this young man's friends want the bug jambalaya

spooned over rice and peas—all except one young man with braids, who says *he* thinks my soup looks more like Northern African food.

"Isn't that North African beans?" he asks.

"North Africa is very near Portugal," I say.

\|\|\| \|\|\| \|\|\|

Anyone with my tendency toward travel does well to take stock of cautionary advisories. "We need to go over into those other racial and ethnic communities," the critic bell hooks said recently, "and we need to speak about what happens when we do, including what makes it hard." But hooks excoriates whites who appropriate black culture in an exploitative fashion, once nearly vaporizing Camille Paglia, who imported some of her sassy style from gay black queens and now goes about enthusing over her rapport with African Americans: "Whooo!" Paglia once gushed. "It's like I feel totally myself." That was too much for hooks, who wrote in response, "Naturally, all black Americans were more than pleased to have Miss Camille give us this vote of confidence, since we *live* to make it possible for white girls like herself to have a place where they can be 'totally' themselves." A similar position is that of Ward Churchill, a Native American writer who is furious that Euro-Americans have presumed to take up Native beliefs. (First you take our land, and now you want our spiritual treasure too.) Neither hooks nor Churchill is lamenting the influences peoples have on one another, which, they well know, can be stopped about as easily as the wind. Rather they are distressed by the ways that power imbalances distort exchanges between peoples.

Closely following the identity debates within the multiracial and African-American communities engages me in thinking not only about how (how much, and if, and where, and why) I may participate in elements of other identities, but about how these social constructions may fare in an emerging transracial society. I find myself seeking out and listening to others grappling with the possibilities of more permeable identities. In *Notes of a White Black Woman*, Judy Scales-Trent proposes that "the difficulty in understanding the notion of ethnicity comes from asking the wrong question all along. The question should not be, 'Where did your people come from?' but rather 'What countries did your people travel through on their way here from Africa?'" And then, recalling the notorious "single drop" rule in America, by which any African ancestry rendered a citizen legally black, Scales-Trent offers a disarming proposal: "Those Americans who call themselves white," she says, "are all pretending to be something else — 'passing' . . . for Mother Africa is mother to us all."

A widely traveled anthropologist is amused by the chameleon nature of her identity. At a conference, she said, "In America, color-coded identities are the norm, so here I am a black woman. But to the South Sea Island tribe I study, all outsiders are *other*, and all others are identified by the word for *white*. Visually, I am close to the islanders' color, but I am an outsider — therefore I am white! In Brazil I am seen as a member of *cultura branca*, white Western culture, as opposed to Afro-Brazilian culture, while in Europe I am perceived, first and foremost, not as black but as an American. Secondly as a woman, third or fourth as a person of African descent. What color am I?" she asked the assembled.

We try all our lives to be human, to know what kind we are. It is not an easy job and it can be encouraging to gather with those who seem like us. It can also be terrifically dangerous—so say the Eastern European poets and writers who have witnessed the power of the group to silence individual conscience, who are trying to warn Americans about investing too much of our identity in any kind of ethnic or cultural tribalism. (Thinking about the recent savagery in the former Yugoslavia, Charles Simic writes: "Here is something we can all count on. Sooner or later our tribe always comes to ask us to agree to murder.")

Even for those of us with just the garden-variety amount of displacement and assimilation, identity is a shifting thing these days. As Jim Sleeper has written, "We are all being 'abducted' from our ancient ethnic moorings by powerful currents we no longer control or fully comprehend." What we will become is unknown, but many who are proud of their origins also value the freedom to claim the elective affinities of which Goethe spoke. It is undeniable that matters of realpolitik power and control underlie and sculpt many aspects of identity. It is undeniable that political and physical survival can be at stake in maintaining strong group identity. But it is also true that for a learning species like ours, which has moved slowly over the globe, gleaning from others is not a denial of native identity but a true and fundamental part of it. Richard Rodriguez delighted and surprised an audience in Miami one winter by saying that it is the Maya Indian in him that loves Shakespeare, the Indian that likes to wear Milanese suits, the Indian that is nimble and adventurous enough to say *"Yo soy chino," "Yo soy italiano," "Yo soy inglés."* (Which, Rodriguez puckishly notes, he is saying in the language of the *conquistadores*.)

I am thinking about these matters when Roots Day is announced—that day each year in late spring when, as Reverend

Brown merrily phrases it, worshippers are invited to come "wearing as much African garb as you have Africa in your heart." This comment is meant to set people with different stylistic preferences at ease, but it might have caused me considerable wardrobe deliberation that first year, except that I forget *which* Sunday is Roots Day, and arrive wearing my usual 1940s-style gray silk suit. But many other people wear their regular outfits, too, including a mainstay of the church, a tall elegant man in his late fifties who arrives wearing his standard double-breasted dark charcoal suit and tie, and is greeted by a woman in the lobby:

"Deacon, is that old suit how much Africa you have in your heart?"

"My sister," he replies easily, "I wore dashikis all *through* the seventies, and to tell you the truth, I am just about *dashikied out.*"

More difficult was the sticky-back label on which we were to write down the name of our root place—"the place you come from," a little sign on the table says. A man next to me writes "Georgia" in magic marker and peels away the backing and presses the label to his chest. Another person is writing "Jamaica." "Gambia" reads another tag. "Congo-Angola." All the tags pointing to history's diasporas and migrations. I stand at the table, pen in hand. Members rustle around the table in an array of African robes, kente cloth, turbans, dashikis—the sisters presenting themselves in what Cornel West names a rich stylization. Deaconess Lillian Allen comes to the table, stands next to me and writes on her label "West Africa and Massachusetts." As she peels off the backing and taps the label smartly onto her dress, she notices my hesitation. She touches my arm lightly, looks me in the eyes and says, "You're home now."

‖‖ ‖‖ ‖‖

Once, for a few weeks, I was completely at home in a place called Aphrodite's Rooms-To-Let. I have been at home walking among Brancusi's polished bronze eggs, hunched over tide pools at the edge of several seas, in red clay fields, and on the eastern shore of Chincoteague, eating blue crabs that my father has caught with a string. Like so many other homes, the one I have found in this community is comforting, quickening, haunting, exquisite, and thorny—sometimes all at once. With one hand I take communion with a congregation, and we are the body together. Meanwhile my other hand is caught in stubborn patterns no individual gesture can undo, most especially the myriad, built-in affirmative action programs for white America, all those privileges so nearly invisible to many whites. Doubtless, too, there are inscapes of understanding that pass me by in these rooms, but on Roots Day, as we stand by the folding cardtable, Deaconess Lillian leaves her hand on my arm a moment longer. "Some things transcend," she says.

And then she must hurry to join the choir, which is readying for its entrance procession—a procession made in a slow, syncopated step, led by a grandmother—a line that can send you into a long meditation on the one and the many. Nearby, Dr. Browning is buttonholing people to buy space in the Men's Fellowship calendar. "For five dollars," he says, "you can put up to five names, birthdays and anniversaries, in the calendar. How many may I put you down for?" Three children run up the carpeted stairs with tambourines in hand.

"Turn to your neighbor," Reverend Brown says when he steps into the pulpit. "Your neighbor is the one next to you," he deadpans. "Say, 'Neighbor,—'"

"Neighbor,—" the word swells up from several hundred congregants amused by their pastor's playful side.

"Neighbor, you look *maaahvelous* this morning."

Reverend Zina Jacque-Bell comes to the pulpit. "And now," she says, "please turn with me to that great old hymn of the church, number 222 in your books, but you won't need your books, you know the words—'We've come this far by faith . . . Oh—Can't turn a-round.' No, we can't turn a-round."

"Everyone who can stand, please stand."

Part Two

ZIP-A-DEE-DO-DAH

E A C H S P R I N G for more than a decade, the canopy of the wild black cherry tree outside my living room window has appealed to a pair of blue jays, the showy bird with a smart crest and black necklace. This year's pair has arrived and the birds are commenced on the days-long project of making a nest, the task for which ornithologists have got the lip-pursing, Felix Unger-ish word "nidification." I'm watching the jays from a living room window thirty feet up in the trees, and I am fluctuating between a quiet panic at having a life so marginal that I can spend most of a day watching blue jays nest and the sense that to observe a bit of creation come close to your window is to be at one of life's hubs. (If by hub I can mean one of those many-faceted jewels that are said to fasten the sprawled net of the world.)

The youngest limbs of the black cherry tree have a smooth, lustrous bark flecked with the ruddy gold nicks called sap stripes. Over time, the swelling cambium layer will cause the young sheath to burst, after which the bark will keep growing, thickening finally into the rough, deckle-edged plates in which the older limbs of the cherry and all of its trunk are clad.

I like this tree of two barks. Its leaves are slender boats — in fall a fleet of yellow. Fully leafed, the wild cherry filters the oblique sun of afternoon in such a way that light shimmers, dances on the walls of our rooms, and makes of a solid something more like water. The tree will also appeal to grackles when the hard green cherries of spring have grown as purple-black as the poison berries of *Grimm's Fairy Tales*. In August, flocks of grackles will come flying to gorge on the cherries, so many landing at once that they shake loose the fruits and cause a steady rain. The sidewalk below will gradually become first a deliquescence of pulp and then, as the cherries rot, a pratfall terrain dotted with hard, ochre pits as round and slick as marbles. Anyone might slip on a pit and fall to a hip operation, so in late summer someone from our house will be out sweeping.

In spring, however, the black cherry belongs to nesting jays. To observe them you must slo-mo to the window, for jays, otherwise so tolerant, will not abide fast or sudden movements. As usual, this year the birds are nesting in a junction where three limbs meet and make a shallow pocket. Everything about this wooden pocket must speak to blue jays, must say in their pattern-language "perfect," much the way we may walk through certain rooms and while speaking of something else — a pocket tidetable, the Bodhisatt-vas — know that we are moving in.

The birds labor over their nest for three days, and they work hard, pausing only to review their construction, to emit their *queedle queedles* and namesake *jeaahs*. A couple building a barbeque over a long weekend, you think, in the decadent nanosecond before you remember your scientific manners. About midway through, when enough material is mounded up, the female jay begins to shape the interior — which she does by plopping herself in the nest, squirming and shifting about in it, pressing and molding everything to the shape of her breast. Whenever the male arrives with more material, she hops out and helps him arrange the new bit. The female also gathers material, but I think she is the only one to fit the nest to her body. I am not sure about that. I am not a student of birds, though I have on occasion traveled with serious birders to blinds and sanctuaries and have watched them (the birders) for many hours and been very moved by their behavior.

But I am going to go out on a limb here, and guess that almost certainly the kind of nest that these blue jays are making has never moved anyone to an encomium to nature's symmetry and perfection. The thing taking shape outside our window is no chambered nautilus shell, with its faultless, secreted spiral of form often invoked when someone wants to take seriously the notion of a great designer—the this-is-all-just-too-exquisite-to-be-random argument. Nor is the blue jay nest a Greek vase of a nest like that of the cliff swallow, whose small-mouthed, jug-like creations hang in clusters under eaves as well as cliffs. The blue jay nest is not a teacup like the nest of the ruby-throated hummingbird, who binds its concoction with threads from spider webs, finishes the outside with lichens, then slicks down its fancy china with saliva. It is not lined in soft wool like the chough's nest. Is not a fey evening bag of a nest like the nest of the Baltimore oriole. It is not a public works project like the nest of the rufous-breasted castle builder, who erects two chambers and a connecting tunnel, or that of the hammerkop, which smoothes eight thousand twigs into a flying-saucer dome strong enough for a man or woman to stand on. The thing outside our window is not even as organized as the lumpen paper wasp's nest which holds a comb of crisp octagons within its bulbous exterior. None of these possibilities for smoothing out chaos have much impressed the blue jay, and at the end of all their labors the jays' nest most resembles a heap of trash.

It is a temporary, provisional architecture made of material plucked from the yards and gutters within a one-block radius, a landscape that is, thanks to a nearby mom & pop store, teeming with the detritus so attractive to a blue jay eye: glinting lottery tickets, popsicle sticks still sticky with grape or orange goo, newspaper twine, and candy wrappers, especially the Kit-Kat with its shook-foil silver lining. The great man of birds placed the blue jay on the same page of his *Guide to Eastern Birds* with the black-billed magpie, the creature of this and that, of making do with scraps.

What it creates is a motley jumble, but the jay is surely guided, no less than the meticulous nautilus, by some inscribed-in-chains-of-nucleic-acid knowledge. So the bricoleurs of the upper canopy know a good heap when they see one. And they know when that heap is fully realized. When it is, the female takes up her residence, and at some point she lays her eggs. During the next few days, for the rare, fleeting moments when she hops off her nest, anyone sitting close by the window and waiting will see four tiny ovals—smooth, with a faint gloss, some years olive in color, other years the blue of a blue-green sea on a partially cloudy day, shadows stippling, speckling the waves.

And does the blue jays' affection for the motley give them an edge in the urban world, an advantage over fussy, fastidious birds like the lazuli bunting? I must ask a serious birder, a man named Emerson Blake and known as Chip (which is not so unlike the *Cyanocitta cristata* being called Jay). The answer from Chip is yes—an elaborate yes which also tells why birds are particular in the first place, why some are disadvantaged by an urban scene, and why some are having a hard time making any nests at all these days. One hard time is illustrated by the spotted owl, a bird who wants peace and quiet and who wants it over an immense territory, over a great big quiet forest. When it does not get it, the bird's endocrine system simply clams up and its hormones cease to deliver the old imperative.

Other birds, Chip tells me, can be fussy about building materials, may not nest at all without the right twig or grass. It's not whim. Absence of the proper materials would be a sign that larger conditions are not right, that the effort to make young would likely fail. Birds that won't breed unless specific materials or foods are present are specialists. The advantage of being a specialist is to thrive in some uncontested niche, to smoke not only one's competitors, but competition itself. Thus Bachman's warbler prevailed in southern canebrakes. Thus the ivory-billed woodpecker lived in virgin pine forests. Thus snail kites in Florida eat only the apple snail, for which purpose they have grown a special beak. The risk can be high, of course, for if canebrake, virgin forest, or apple snails disappear, the specialist is, as Chip puts it, "out of business."

That was the fate of the dusky seaside sparrow, perfectly adapted to certain tidal salt marshes along the Florida coast, and not counting on Cape Canaveral or the draining of the marshes for mosquito control. A little planning could have spared the niche of this sparrow (whose name alone is worth sparing), but a bird like the California condor, whose idea of what Southern California should be is profoundly at odds with what Southern California has become, can probably no longer survive without perpetual human assistance.

My birds, the blue jays outside the window, are neither specialists nor maladapted to this century. Blue jays are the most general of generalists. More intelligent than many birds, they are able to withstand competition on several fronts, and if out-maneuvered, they think nothing of taking up life in another site. "The blue jay," Chip muses, "is almost too adaptable." By which he means, he explains, that the success of generalists can mask the demise of specialists, who have the more sensitive bonds to place. Birdwatchers like Chip know what once existed, and they miss it. The way you may feel at a McDonald's if you remember the diner that had red-eye gravy.

Adaptability, however, is what allows blue jays to nest on the margins of an industrial metropolis, and I am glad for that. Naturally I gasp at the colorful gems of rural glades—the rufous breasteds, the golds, the waxwinged, cerulean, and painted. But on this street, where the airborne population is pigeons, grackles, and the occasional blimp, the blue jay passes for beauty. And although I (who require *petit pain* for breakfast, classic-style, *not* sourdough, who will go miles for red-eye gravy) am much in sympathy with the specialists, I do study the blue jay's resiliency: this is the bird of the postmodern, of invention and recycling, of found art.

Above all, this is the bird that comes to our window. It comes like the puppy that toddles across the room from the cardboard birthing box, puts its head in your lap, and chooses you. When life come to you like that, you refuse it at your own peril. So I am partisan to the jays, and root for their eggs. And however successful in the larger picture, here jay eggs are greatly endangered by the Visigoths of the urban forest—the bushy-tailed gray destroyers who travel the telephone cables and who can turn a nest of eggs into yellow slime in less time than it takes to say "Great Geometer of the Void," less time than it takes to see Samuel Beckett's *Breath*. (The action: curtain rise; cry and one breath; curtain fall.)

It can be just that minimalist, that swift and iconic with these nests. Sometimes a nursery, sometimes a bare choir. In ruin, however, the blue jays do not stand around in stunned silence, they do not reel between the great equanimity where all is balance, and the small, immediate realm where they have been roughed up. They do not mull the more-than-human scheme of justice, variously felt as a benevolence whose eye is on the sparrow, as a magisterial indifference, as a mocking voice in a whirlwind. They just fly away, on those coveted wings.

Eggs, they know very well, are fair game in the gulping world. The eager mouth of the ocean swallows most of its own children, and, it turns out, the blue jay's own favorite food is other bird's eggs. "Trash birds," says another of my bird-world informants, "like the roughnecks of Dickensian London, doing whatever they can to get by, and not thinking much about the ethics of it. Not pretty." (Do Americans deny that class exists so that we can have the fun of projecting it onto flora and fauna?) Well, obviously I do not defend the jays' eating other bird's eggs. They should stop, and should eat more bright-orange and leafy green vegetables, more soy, less fat. And I honestly don't know what trashy things the blue jays do when not by our window being hard-working postmodernists or brooding on their four cloudy-sea eggs, conveying warmth through the ovals, being brave, warm, patient, being all that parents can be, settling over the delicate shells just so. Let's just say that when a creature lays four speckled eggs close by your house, you like for those eggs to hatch.

Because the odds for our local blue jays' eggs are always longish, I root for them with a certain kind of hope. Not the usual sort, which is desire combined with expectation, or even expectation *without* desire—sheer prospect. But the kind of hope that seasoned fans have for the Red Sox and the Cubs, a brand of hope far from pie-eyed optimism, closer to the state of mind that the French call *une douce resignation*. In our new world, the adjective that most often appears before "resignation" is "bitter." But *une douce resignation* is not the defeated mood so repugnant to the American spirit. Although it is of course resigned to the fact that the world is, as Margaret Thatcher put it the week she was (hooray) booted out, "a funny old world," this mood is *douce*—sweet—from kindness and time, says a Belgian poet friend, who also says that if Americans are too doggedly, even eerily optimistic for *une douce resignation* (she doesn't know about baseball), her people, the Flemish, are too taciturn for it. The mood rises most in southern France, in Corsica, also in Italy and Spain, and a Buddhist friend tells me that it is very close to his practice of detachment—a way that fuses passionate caring and letting be, a way of existing within the world's own quite motley assembly of nests, violence, and summer games.

This year's nest is a beauty, an extravagant assembly, a miniature L. A. Watts Tower of a nest, a work that might make Joseph Cornell smile. *Regardez:* A few twigs for a foundation. Then snippets of fine green, and red, and black telephone wire. A yellow plastic garbage-bag tie. Another layer of twigs. A Doublemint gum wrapper. Some shreds of computer paper. Some weeds. Part of a pre-tied drugstore bow. With binoculars, I can see that the birds have incorporated most of the label of a good Beaujolais, George de Boeuf's Brouilly, 1995. The *piece de résistance*, the thing over which the birds have queedled and queedled, is a plastic picnic fork; over the course of two hours, they have gotten it angled into one side of the nest, with the tines pointed outwards, bristling like a pitchfork.

Something to make the destroyer pause? It is a large white fork, a piece of debris that came, I will guess, either from Marcella's on the avenue (which makes the Classico sandwich of prosciutto sliced to translucency) or from the House O' Pizza, where they will, if you ask, make a meatless, cheeseless sub with all the condiments, a delicacy that Sal and I have settled on calling a Nothing With Everything.

HOUSE

〽〽〽   〽〽〽   〽〽〽

ALREADY, my father had won one feather boa that night. When his second ticket number was also called, and he walked onto the stage again, Pearl Bailey leaned her husky voice into the microphone.

"Darlin'," she cooed, "how many times are you going to come up here to see me?"

My father, a quiet man, replied, "As many times as you call out my name, Miss Bailey, I'll come up."

Knowing my father, I know that his answer was commonsensical, a matter-of-fact statement about what he would do, but in the moment, in the ballroom, it sounded saucy and courtly, obedient and flirtatious. Pleased, Pearl Bailey kissed my father and looped the second boa around his neck. He went, flushed, back to his table to rejoin my mother.

A few months later, at a time when I was planning a move, my mother called to say, "Your father and I have decided that your life is more a feather-boa life than ours," and that they were making me a gift of the larger of the two creatures. Mine had never been an *especially* feather-boa life—didn't the last one occur in the 1920s, and didn't it involve ocean liners, and champagne in high heels?—but I understood that my mother and father were sending me a life accessory, and I treated the boa as if it might be needed.

On the day of the move, standing on the balcony of the new third-floor flat, I chanced to see the moving man scoop the length of feathers from the seat of his cab and start up the walk with it. I began to call out to him, "I'll come down and get that," and then I didn't. The mover was a very strong man, but strength is not what is required for handling a large feather boa, whose morphology is unlike that of a cardboard box. The moving man was having some trouble containing the whole slithery mass in his arms, and keeping the plumes from slinking along the ground. I was impressed, though, that he had not shrunk from attempting the thing, and by the time he had walked up three flights of stairs, he had solved the problem of moving a boa. He was wearing it.

He knew what to call it, too.

"Where do you want your boa?" the mover asked when he had gotten the accessory through the door. His voice was muffled, his face, shoulders, and chest all hidden, swallowed in feathers. But I had noticed that he had dark amber eyes, a loping walk, that he exuded a cat-like sense of ease, of finding the effortless path through any room. At the end of the day, the mover sat down on a carton and drank a glass of water.

"It's not just lifting," he said, making conversation.

I said something, and the mover said, "It's not like weight-lifting, it's about putting weight in motion. There was one guy I worked with for three years, and we could make things move like water. It's like getting in the groove when you're playing music, and it is satisfying to be an agent of change."

I must have said something in reply, and although it would be a while before we understood, the moving man and I had begun what Auden named "the long conversation," the one whose fascinations last. Most of the conversation—our married life—has been conducted in that top-floor flat of a triple-decker.

⦚⦚⦚   ⦚⦚⦚   ⦚⦚⦚

A triple-decker, for those unfamiliar with Boston's housing stock, is an indigenous, late-nineteenth-century design that stacks three identical apartments and wraps them in an envelope of shingles, porches, railings, and columns, so that the imposing front facade resembles a tiered cake or domestic temple for the American worker.

Sometimes the columns are Corinthian, sometimes neo-Colonial, and there are triple-deckers of distinction, with marble mantles and parquet floors, but the great bulk of them are immensely plain, the variations among them on the order of one twin having more freckles than the other, or one having green-gray eyes, the other gray-green. The original idea for this house-type was a single owner who afforded the whole thing by renting out the other two flats, but recently many triple-decker houses, like ours, have been converted into condominiums.

It is not a perfect house. Our flat is so compact that we must treat it as sailors do a boat, using every cranny, pressing each room into double-duty, jettisoning often. In any high wind the house will sway, and it shivers when temblors roll down from the glacial hills in whose bowl our city rests. Triple-decker dwellers must worry more than most homeowners about roof leaks because the flat roofs are designed to slope inwards toward a central drainpipe that funnels rainwater through the interior of the house; it is one thing to gracefully, wisely yield to nature, and another to actually tempt her great storms, invite them into your house.

But the light up here is redemptively good, and from the windows in the western bay there is a clear view of the granite hills. In the evening, the windows frame the book of light: shameless magentas, smoky grays, aboriginal blues crossed by contrails of jets. Not long after our triple-decker was built, someone had the good sense to plant two trees: a Norway maple that buckles up the sidewalk and rises fifty feet close by the house facade, shading the front porch and balconies; and, on the western face, the wild black cherry, the sometime home of jays. Situated in the two canopies, the top floor flat feels like a treehouse.

It is a hard proposition to offer about a house in a time when many seem uncertain if we ourselves have souls (in what used to be called our soul-cases), yet anyone who has loved a house may agree that not only do we infuse our houses with the steady sedimentations of home, but that houses have some spirit of their own, which they, by a silent, steady appeal, infuse in us.

\|\|\| \|\|\| \|\|\|

Triple-deckers emerged in our city in the 1880s, rising up in great clusters. Sixteen thousand of them by one count. The strands in their creation story are several, among them the safety and construction codes that the Massachusetts legislature enacted in 1874, prodded by gangs of do-right Boston women. The new codes, which applied to all buildings for more than three families, were intended to transform Boston's ghastly tenement slums; but because the new standards would increase construction costs, local builders and speculators were reluctant to risk overpricing the market, and soon realized that they could finesse the codes altogether by building a house for *just* three families.

In his elegant book *Built in Boston*, Douglass Shand Tucci delves more deeply into the origin of the triple-decker and observes that something else was also at work. At the same time that the construction code legislation was passed, streetcar lines were being extended out of the city, enabling lower-middle-income families to move to the inner suburbs. "What has been widely overlooked," Tucci writes, "is that the three-decker as a building type, at all class levels, is the streetcar-suburb version, on the detached town house streetscape, of the French flat apartment house." To Tucci's eye, the plain houses are stripped-to-the-bone versions of an opulent style borrowed, from Paris, for the fashionable streets of America. Known locally as family or apartment hotels, the first French flat was the Hotel Pelham in 1857, followed by the Agassiz, Cluny, Somerset, and Oxford, to name only a few, and the *ne plus ultra*, the Hotel Vendome. As streetcar suburbs continued to grow around the core city, architects began experimenting with the French flat form, scaling it to the new suburban streetscape. These designers were not contemplating the needs of working-class persons, but their gracious, multi-family houses may have been a clue to those who were.

A third strand of the emergence story is suggested by my neighbor, the urban geographer Arthur Krim, who reasonably points out that the French flat did not have either the front *piazzas* or the back service porches that characterized the new triple-decker house—and something else did. One day as we are walking together down the main street through this neighborhood, Arthur stops in front of a blue three-story house built by nineteenth-century French-Canadian carpenters in the style of Maritime fishermen's houses.

This house, says Arthur, with its exterior stairway and ample porches on each landing (good places for gear, boots, and fish), is his candidate for the triple-decker prototype.

All the stories agree that the triple-decker is a building of the vernacular. The word is as nice on the tongue as *Pinnochio* and *funicular*, and it means, of course, the colloquial, most peculiarly native language of a particular locality or people. Architects, who have long taken the metaphor of language as a way to talk about their art (window "idioms," visual "quotations"), use "vernacular" to refer to the local dialect of built form. Recently the vernacular has been admired as a regional stay against the homogenous, but there can also be a disparaging note, like that sounded by the author G. G. Scott in *Remarks Secular and Domestic*, who, in 1857, wished to "call attention to the meanness of our vernacular architecture, and to the very partial success which has attended the attempts at its improvement."

The triple-decker villas of the vernacular, however, were far more than a partial success. Families instantly preferred them to the large tenement buildings of Boston, whose conditions had moved observers to use the word "Calcutta." By contrast, the triple-decker was a house of bread and roses: windows on all four sides; balconies in front for taking the air; the back service porch for training a grape vine, for flying laundry, for conversing with neighbors or politely ignoring them. In some sections of our metropolis these plain Janes line the streets for blocks and blocks—voluminous numbers of them standing shoulder to shoulder, sometimes borrowing a little style from the fashionable brick bow-fronts, such as the one built by Howells's parvenu paint king, Silas Lapham, as he roared first toward collapse, then rise.

The first name for the triple-decker house, "three-decker,"

seems a simple, descriptive phrase, but it has a past. "Three-decker" was laudatory, naval lingo for England's great gunboats, the sovereigns of the sea each bristling with three decks of cannon. In America, the term came to signify anything of size or importance—a lavish dinner menu, words of Latin or Greek derivation, a formidable woman, or a bit of orthodoxy could be "three-decker." Any actually tri-partite thing, such as a skirt with three flounces, was a candidate, and "three-decker" was a perfect name—a visual pun, really—for the hulking, three-story houses whose stacked porches must have recalled the decks of a nineteenth-century warship. It may also have been slightly satirical, for certainly these dwellings never shared in the glory heaped on the men-o'-war. The houses were often sneered at as a "blight" and "Boston's weed." Even Lewis Mumford, lover of cities, sniffed at them: "Vast wooden firetraps," he lamented, though he did notice that triple-deckers are "happily blessed with open-air porches."

Ours is at least a sturdy weed, built in 1924, near the end of the era, by Jeremiah McCarthy and Alfred Tremblay. The house is solid, if slightly flexible, and like most of its kind it has a carpenter's sense of the primacy of wood. Even the most modest triple-decker has built-in wooden china cabinets, pantries, and bay windows. No opportunity was missed to put wood trim or molding around something—a recessed hutch, a mirror, a bookcase. Doors also call for moldings and that may be why there are so many doors in our triple decker—and in such close proximity that our flat could easily serve as the set for a play that involves five or six characters darting in and out of rooms, yearning to embrace, strangle, deceive, adore, or amuse each other.

|||| |||| ||||

By the time Peter and I came on stage, the wallpaper in the living room was five layers deep. Peeling back one brittle corner, I had the old wish that the former sounds of the house had been absorbed—transduced and stored in the walls rather than passing through them in waves. If only the dragon-like steamer whose hot plate was loosening reluctant layers of patterned paper could also release the sounds of the house—like the spring melt once released cries and howls of a previous winter's battle to Baudelaire's travelers. (The battle sounds, he explained, had frozen in the ice.) We were able to scrape off four of the five wallpapers—the dark flower, an unfortunate op art print, the Chinese junks, the nosegays. The last layer, a sober stripe, had become one with the plaster.

The walls were silent, but the day we tore down the old coal bin in the basement, the house did offer up a name. The former bin was filled with black anthracite dust, and, we feared, stray asbestos fibers from a crumbling oil burner. Cleaning away the suspect rubble, we found two yellowed pieces of paper tacked to a slat. One was an electrical bill from 1928 for two dollars and fifteen cents, and the other, just a scrap, a corner of a coal delivery note. Both bills were made out to Granchelli—the name and the sums written in the fine spidery script of a world in which Penmanship was an important school subject.

Some months later, I went to the Middlesex County Courthouse, which houses the Registry of Deeds. Deeds since the 1930s are kept in a cavernous room filled with high stools and the kind of slant-top desks that Bob Cratchit hunched over before Scrooge had his epiphanies. The vast floor is a tile mosaic with bands of vegetable motifs, laid by Italian artisans. The perimeter of the hall is filled by steel shelves of bound volumes, and with phalanxes of women typing. Citizens standing on the mezzanine catwalk and looking down on the beehive below might well think of Alexandria and Rome, other great recording cities.

From eight in the morning until four in the afternoon, the Registry of Deeds hums with paralegals doing title searches, homeowners digging for tax comparisons. A woman follows a shard of information about an eighteenth-century cemetery. Pols buttonhole one another. At one end of the room stands a booth staffed by two clerks who answer questions in the polite but war-weary monotones of civil servants who have seen and heard too much, who can no longer be vaguely interested in anyone's quest: "Grantor Index, not Grantee," one says to me firmly. "Title filing only," warns a clerk who sees me getting dangerously close to her post.

The immense bound volumes of deeds are stored on long metal shelves, and the passages between the shelves are like lanes through a bookish village. In a series of soft, sage-gray clothbound books with marbled, maroon endpapers I can follow the trail of our house through the twentieth century. The books hold by-laws, mortgages, and quitclaims—the kinds of papers that tell the leanest, most official version of lives, in the way an annual tax accounting is, and is not, the story of a year. By a series of interlocking numbers, each document refers a researcher to relevant collateral documents, and in the case of a real estate sale, to the immediately preceding sale. Two deeds later (or rather, earlier), I have been sent to a book so old that it is kept in a vault in the cool courthouse basement.

Volumes in the basement are guarded by a silent, round man who, upon request, will bear a book from out the closeted stacks, lumbering with it resting on his shoulder, Atlas-fashion. The woman in front of me in line cannot figure out the next step in a search that has taken her back to the year 1825. "I couldn't say," says the clerk. "You're at a dead end," he adds, in the flat voice of someone who knows what one feels like.

Many of the volumes down here are handwritten ledger pages, each transaction entered in a flowing, elegant script, a measured, serene hand. But the high school boy next to me at the table groans at a page from 1823 which is nothing but crabbed globs.

"History report," he says to me, pulling a face.

"About what?" I ask.

"Some dead guy," the boy replies.

Seven people sit in this sepulchral basement, at two tables, each of us poring over a volume. We make a small, instant society, travelers poking like snails through years. The walls of the basement room are solid book, and each book holds clues, fragments of countless stories, which will speak only if touched by someone's love or curiosity or need. In the 1925 volume I come upon the title for the Granchellis' three-family house: it was purchased, I see, from the local builders McCarthy and Tremblay, for eight thousand dollars, and the Granchellis' first names were Felix and Juanita.

||| ||| |||

Hints and sensations still fluoresce from time to time when we stumble on something in a basement corner or flattened under a cabinet: a brass switchplate, a half-roll of wallpaper, the faint rose smell in the china hutch where a strong perfume must have spilled. And once I found an unopened package of All Purpose Rit Tint & Dye that—judging from the price, 20¢, bravely printed on the package—Juanita Granchelli must have bought in the 1950s. The relic is soft, and granules of dye still plump the manila envelope. The box contains a folder of instructions: cartoon drawings of an aproned woman smiling rhapturously as she tints a blouse aqua in her sink / dyes it in a pan on the stove / colors it in her washing machine. An even older artifact surfaced: a McCall's pattern kit for cross-stitch designs, which sold for ten cents. The tissue paper is printed with designs for trimming children's dresses, rompers, pockets of aprons. There is a squirrel design, and a bear with a candlestick. "The four swimming ducks are especially cunning for a towel," the packet says, and as for the wolf: "A dash of red in his eye, and a red tongue, will make him look quite natural." Well. I could hardly throw these things away, and the most likely place for them was in a box along with my grandmother's gold umbrella handle, her writing pen, my father's U.S. Army Second Infantry pin.

〳〳〳〳   〳〳〳〳   〳〳〳〳

Next to the Granchellis' title in the Registry book there is an informal, marginal entry, made in a later hand, in brown ink. The referent number sends me back upstairs, to a page in modern-era book, an entry made in the early fifties: Felix Tocco Granchelli. Born in Italy. A tailor. Died June 5th, of bronchial pneumonia. Buried in the parish cemetery. The documents in this collection also tell me that his wife continued to live in her triple-decker for another twenty-five years after her husband's death, and that in the 1970s her sons, "conservators of Juanita Noble Granchelli," sold her house, releasing all rights of dower and homestead.

I suppose they were very different from us. They raised two boys in rooms that now seem barely able to hold two adults, our teapots, cameras, books, amplifiers, our mustards, bags of rice. The interior layout has changed since the Granchellis lived here. We sleep in their former front parlor, watch *Wings of Desire* and *Tampopo* on video where they dined, dine where they kept canned goods and dustbins, store the works of Orwell, Lao Tsu, Raboteau, and Elizabeth Bishop where they kept china. But we share an intimate, corporeal knowledge with the first and longest inhabitants of this house. Our predecessors knew the exact patterns of light we know: the cool grey brightness of the northern rooms, the full-bodied summer sun tracking across the southern porch, then stealing into the kitchen windows after one o'clock, slanting by late afternoon onto the oak plank floor, making it the color of jarred honey. They looked out on the rough-barked cherry, saw its crooks fill with snow in winter, observed the crows who swim and soar through the sodden-cotton skies of winter. By the Eisenhower era, Mrs. Granchelli out for a walk would have seen the Broadway-bulb marquee of the discount liquor store (as brilliant as zircons), and she would have seen the pale yellow-green fluorescence of the Kevin L. Lynch VFW sign—on a foggy day, the most radiant thing on the street. In all eras, they would have seen the liquidities of evening, a woman walking home in that warm light, her face the color of the sky. They would have heard the train whistle sounding through that color, and seen a spider, a shaggy holiness meditating on the wall. When did it arrive?

Their bodies knew what ours know: how to move down the narrow hall with a basket of laundry, how to ease into the enameled clawfoot tub, lower one's back slowly against the cool porcelain above the warm water line. They saw light explode on the glass pane of the bath window, the glass etched to resemble fernlike frost swirls. They heard footfalls echoing up and down the uncarpeted stairwell, the hiss of radiators dispensing heat, the rattle and hammering clank when a bubble of air is caught in the pipes, the low whistles, little sighs, gurgles, clicks, the *psssauaunghg psssauaunghg* of steam rising and finding release. They saw the quick, feathery shadows and projections that travel at night over the ceilings when the beams of a passing car flash through the window. They were awakened by the smart, clear moons of December, hopeful in the cold, the moon's startled face.

|||| |||| ||||

One morning on the balcony of the vernacular villa, I sat reading Colette's hymn to her mother, Sido, and her childhood home in Saint-Sauveur. Sun was sculpting the columns of the balcony, one side a clear face, the other shadowed. A large green insect with lacy wings was breathing hard on the wall. I cannot say for sure, but if I were to win the lottery with one of the Set For Life tickets that I occasionally buy at the corner store, I might be one of those people who say "We'll stay where we are." It was the poet George Starbuck who first brought this rhetorical gesture to my attention. Someone had just won jillions in the state lottery and George, peerless student of American talk, was not happy. He was not happy about the way the new winner was talking to reporters. She had said the standard thing, something like, "Fred and I are going to stay in our same house, keep our same jobs at the lint factory, drive the same car. It's not going to change anything." George had heard this sort of American lottery-winner talk once too often. Someone, he fumed — namely the Lottery Commissioner — should have the authority to step in whenever a new winner says that nothing will change upon the influx of all that green, and reply, "Well then *give it back.*"

Winning the lottery, George Starbuck told me that day, is supposed to change your life.

Naturally, another house, another place, would have its own generosities. But who does not grow wary of adding to the burden of vanished things? And this is the place where our eyes have long opened on the light brightening behind the massed maples to the east. This is the place where we know the mail carrier's name, U Wong Woo—where U Wong (who asks us to call him Kevin) sits on our shady porch to eat his lunch. This is the place where I first began to honor the intersection of will and world, to admire the contours of existence as one admires the precise lines and shapes of a lifemask. "Wyre" the medievals named it: what has actually come to pass, what *is* as opposed to all that might be—and the root of our word "weird."

WATERSHED

AN EXCURSION IN FOUR PARTS

〳〳〳   〳〳〳   〳〳〳   〳〳〳   〳〳〳   〳〳〳   〳〳〳   〳〳〳   〳〳〳

The idea of nature as a well-balanced machine has been replaced by complicated talk of dynamic and multiple equilibriums, chaotic systems, and other unsettling notions that undermine all the conditioning we received at the hands of Disney nature films and Mark Trail comic strips. Nature, we are learning, is enormously untidy and rarely predictable. Change is the rule, stability the exception.

—Paul Schullery, *Searching for Yellowstone*

STREET

Like travelers hoping to keep some rare place unknown, new residents will whisper "There's nothing else like this in the city," and visitors who chance upon, or manage to navigate into, the neighborhood are surprised. They remark on the hush, on the colonnade of maples whose canopies have grown together into a continuous arch, on the small, close-set houses with front porches (which older residents call their *piazzas*)—on the overall sense of being in a little village. Maybe a fishing village on some out-of-the-way peninsula.

It is a small urban enclave in the late Tip O'Neill's lunch-bucket liberal district—a neighborhood on the very edge of the city, on land that was briefly a race course, land that held our city's poor

128

house and its bone factory (whatever that is, and I'm not sure I want to know). The earliest inhabitants in the modern era were predominantly French-Canadians from the Madeleine Islands, Nova Scotia, and Quebec. Immigrants from other countries were lightly represented along the street, among them Felix and Juanita Granchelli, the former inhabitants of our house, from Italy and Spain respectively. But this enclave was Little France, the French-Canadian concentrate, while streets immediately surrounding it were home to Irish and West Indian immigrants, and African Americans, many migrated from the South. Together, the varied people of this end of town created a way of life based on dogged work, devotion, donuts from Verna's coffee shop, tolerance, some booze, lots of church, and church bingo, and sitting on their piazzas talking to one another in the evenings. "Sitting out," they called it. At the end of a road, and on the edge of town, the neighborhood was a modest backwater: "No one came down here unless they lived here," says my neighbor Alice, who started living here herself seventy-four years ago, when she was two. But Speaker O'Neill took the local, big-hearted ethos national, where it made a difference across the land.

The bones of the early demographics of this street are still visible where mailboxes read Beauchemin, Arsenault, Grenier, Ouellette, but the area is now also home to citizens from India, Jamaica, Haiti, China, Cape Verde, and to northern European *mestizos* like myself. It is still a quiet enclave, some of the quiet engineered by a rabbit warren of one-way streets that deters most incidental traffic from attempting the neighborhood, creating a precinct that is, for a city, positively serene. By day you can hear the tinkle of a small brass bell tied to the door of the mom & pop across the street; by night, the driving, lightly syncopated jazz of crickets and katydids.

Not too quiet, though. The bells of St. John the Evangelist peel on the quarter hour, and Notre Dame de Pitié rings its three great Belgian-made *cloches* (named Joseph, Marie, and Jesus). By Verdin Bell recordings, Notre Dame also plays melodies, and in season, the carols *"Venez Divin Messie"* and *"Dans Cette Étable."* Daily a train whistle sounds its minor key, round as a Wurlitzer organ, and teenagers sometimes roil along the sidewalk at night releasing barbaric yawps.

Oh, *way* beyond yawps, my husband Peter reminds me. Completely over the top in the case of the five teenage girls with boomboxes who, one spring morning at three A.M., brought many sleepy and irate citizens onto our balconies. When it was suggested that the young banshees lower their volumes and go home, the girls used an old Anglo-Saxon word and showed us how very much louder their radios could go. (I have to say, I was a tiny bit proud of the girls.) In the late afternoons, younger children come by our house: girls in pleated, plaid skirts, often singing; boys whose leitmotif is the plump sound of a basketball bounced along the pavement—louder, louder, then fading—sounding all the way to the hoop in the corner park, where on any given summer day the wading pool is full of toddlers whose sleep-deprived parents confer on nearby benches. And recently there is a brand-new sound.

The brand-new sound arrives about nine o'clock on summer evenings. You can hear it coming several blocks away, crawling closer, growing louder until—as it passes our house—it is an earth-rumbling, glass-rattling sound, a rhythmic, ultra-low-frequency pulse, emanating not from a volcano, not from a shifting tectonic plate, but from a car. Peter, the musician, explains it to me.

"Well, it's kind of a guy thing," he says, which much I had

guessed. To achieve the effect, a guy, usually a young one of seventeen or eighteen, retrofits his car with several high-powered amplifiers—one for treble, one for bass, as well as additional amplifiers for each channel. He also installs a couple of large, industrial-strength Bazooka brand loudspeakers, and hooks it all up to a CD player and tape deck. The resulting system is intended for a single kind of music, a kind called house music (though it would seem to have as little to do with a house as possible), which is a subset of rap.

"House music," Peter says, "is long dance jams of sampled loops and effects, heavily percussive, with huge bass sounds created by combined synthesized and electric bass, and drum machines. A common technique," Peter continues, unfazed by my wondering gaze, "is to have two or three drum sounds all hitting at the same time. That gives a fatter, chord-like sound from the drums. What they have learned is that if you take a plain eighty- or one-hundred-cycle tone, and hook it up so that it triggers simultaneously with a kick drum, it gives a massive low end."

"Are they trying to attract girls?"

"Well, sure," Peter replies. "But on some level they're trying to impress everybody. They want people to notice, to say 'There goes Rudy, he's got the loudest car in the neighborhood.' It's like hot-rodding a car, only instead of speed you're looking for more noise, more bass. They like to stop at lights, meet at certain places, sort of joust to see who can make the most booming sound—'n' stuff."

The house-music crowd has Peter, the ur-grammarian, the man who can fume about a misplaced modifier on the evening news, saying "'n' stuff." But does such fast, driving sound work on girls? On girl katydids it does. The journal *Nature* has reported that the rhythmic night chirruping of male katydids, the resonant sound which the males accomplish by rubbing their front wings together, is not a cooperative effort. Though it sounds like one of nature's most harmonious sing-alongs, the buggy nocturne in our summer grasses is the by-product of an intense competition. Researchers have found that males who can chirp only a few thousandths of a second ahead of others attract, in the words of the scientists, "most of the females."

I admit to being attracted to what Walt Whitman calls the hum of a valved voice, to the sound of my husband's voice reading Wodehouse's pitch-perfect comedy, to Alberta Hunter singing "I'll be down to get you in a taxi, Honey — Honey, don't be late, I want to be there when the band starts playing," and endlessly to the E-flat Trio, the passage where Schubert mourns Beethoven. And it is true that I hear the massive low end fleetingly, for a few minutes, once or twice a night. But it sends me to realize what these boys are up to: as the big hulk of the metallic car body vibrates, the whole vehicle serves as a resonating shell for sound. That is, *the whole car has been turned into an instrument.* Slipping through the night in their throaty, big-talking drums, these boys are *broadcasting.*

Not far from this urban lyric, there is a lumberyard, a Big & Tall men's shop, two grand churches, and two fortune-telling parlors. There is a genetics lab in our neighborhood, close to a Tex-Mex bar and grill where any escaping DNA on the lam could hide for days. There are fishmongers, lobster tanks, and think tanks here, and a storefront dental office with a neon molar in the window. There is a candy jobber and the Free Romania Foundation. There used to be a fast-food shack, name of Babo's, with a sweeping roof to die for, a pure Brancusi bird blown off its flyway and landed on a local sub shop. There are sushi bars with sandalwood counters, and pizza parlors, and, all of a sudden, nail salons (four of them where before there were no nail salons and we all got by without anyone once saying "I'd give anything for a decent pedicure"—so who supports these places, and why? Must find out).

It is a dense, urban neighborhood, baroque with energies, more than anyone could ever say. Just last year we were all surprised to hear that a call-girl ring was operating in a house not far from ours—and the people who ran it were "very polite," the neighbors said. Even more surprising, to me, was the discovery that many parts of this neighborhood and its many activities take place on land that was—not so very long ago—a vast and ancient swamp.

SWAMP

It was situated a little north of the clam flats along the Charles River, about nine miles inland from the coast. The Great Swamp it was named by the earliest English settlers to ink its features on their maps: acres of a glacially sculpted meander, slow streams and ponds, humpbacked islands that rose from shallow pools fringed by reeds, brackish marshes that were home to heron rookeries, wild rices, fishes, and pied-billed grebes. For some ten thousand years, this fertility was stung with sun, was giddy with births and deaths, was preening, humming, and hungry.

The conditions for a swamp of such magnitude emerged as the last North American glacier melted and retreated, and the whole basin of our region became a shallow inland lake—an embayment contained by surrounding drumlin hills. Most locally, the waters were corralled by a recessional moraine whose gentle bulk still slants across our city, and by beds of impervious blue clays under the gravel and watery surface. The first human beings to arrive in this watershed found vegetated marshes and swampland sprawling around two medium-big bodies of water—one of which is the amoebal-shaped place we call Fresh Pond.

I have lived close to Fresh Pond for most my adult life, and had frequented its shores for years before I knew a single thing about the former swamp, although I suppose I would have said that *something* must have existed where now sits a megaplex cinema and the market where Michael runs the cheese department and sets aside small, ripe reblochons that delight my husband. Never, I think, would I have guessed that the shopping plaza and its hardtop parking lot were formerly a red maple swamp, distinctive acres within the larger swamp, with smatterings of rum cherries and tupelo trees, with water lilies, pickerel weed, and high-bush blueberries— "overrun," said one habitué, in vines of flowering clematis.

Shortly after learning of this former reality, I had occasion to drive to the Staples office supply store at the shopping mall. There, walking across the parking lot, I noticed my mind half trying to believe that if we could jackhammer up the asphalt, underneath we would find—oh, not entire squashed maples and blueberry bushes, but some incipient elements of a swamp, some boggy fen, or fenny bog, a slough or quagmire, marshy sponge or squishy mud—the whole exchanging, liquid world lost to the single, dry, abrupt syllable: *mall*.

In truth, I like the mall, or at least I don't stay away. Its makers thought little of shadow and light, of coincidence, learned nothing of design from once watching a bird fold its wings, but the mall serves up shelves of the excellent Pilot pen, of shampoo with conditioner mixed right in, of Maxell audio tapes in five-packs. There are birds-of-paradise to be found at this mall, and a newspaper vending box whose simple door opens on papers resting inside in a trusting stack. I also have reason to admire the nearby grid of transformer towers carrying cables that step down the voltage from the North-east grid to a pulse our local wires can handle. There is a word to be said for the cement-block home of Intermetrix (whatever that is, there are eight gold ballroom-dancing trophies on the sill of one of the company windows, with eight gold couples spinning on top), and another word for the family-style restaurant that squats over a one-time rookery serving desserts with galactic names—Starstruck Sundae, Chaos Pie—and way too much whipped cream from a pressurized can.

Certainly by middle age one knows that ours is a paradoxical par-adise, that all times, all lands, all selves are an alloy of scar and grace, that blight may turn to beauty and beauty to blight, like mis-chievous changelings teasing the stolid. Certainly we know that our land is one supple carnival of misrule, a mesh of redemptive improbability and change. Still, this particular news—a whole drop-dead gorgeous swamp gone missing—hit me hard, for I am very partial to swamps. My mother was conceived in one, and I have the gene for growing quiet before the lines spun out from some orb spider's holy gut, for watching wading birds resemble Yuan dynasty works on silk. The Great Swamp of this region was also a sponge, a nursery, and an aeration—and it presents my mind with a nice conundrum to know that a neighborhood I cherish was its demise.

Perhaps I brooded over the great lost swamp because I had at-tained an age when sympathy for vanished things comes easily, when we are aware of mortality as real and not some absurd con-cept that has, in any event, nothing to do with ourselves, our only parents, our irreplaceable friend. Certainly I was beginning to like the past more as people, places, and ambitions receded into it, became its populace. And perhaps that is why I began to go out walking on long tours across the urban moors of one edge city, circumnavigating the former contours of a swamp, seeking its remnants.

As it turns out, a glacial work is hard to eradicate entirely. It is true that we are not going to find any quick phosphorescence of life under the asphalt slabs, because the lowland environ of this fringy area has been the place where, for several hundred years, townspeople have seen fit to locate everything from almshouses to latex plants. But vestiges of the Great Swamp survive in patches: in the trickle of brook through a maintenance yard, flanked in spring by tall gray pussywillow wands; in a slippery gully of jewelweed; in a patch of riverine marsh; in wet basements and yellow-limbed willows. Nor am I the only one to spot the remains. Nine great blue herons spend weeks on the river that runs alongside the think tank, not far from the grounds where male woodcocks perform their spiraling courtship flights. Wild Saint-John's-wort, healer of melancholy, grows here, also tansy and yarrow, *Achillea millefolium*, the spicy-smelling plant that sooths wounds—recently introduced species mingling with older ones. There are killdeer, muskrat, and ring-necked pheasants (the last a twentieth-century arrival) not far from the commuter trains, and against all odds, alewife fishes which manage to run in the spring as they have for millennia, coming upriver from their ocean home to spawn in the dwindling freshwater streams of our watershed. Here and there, in a secluded patch of these old wilds, it is possible to get lost.

And one late afternoon as I was driving home on a road that passes a mucky pond just behind the Pepperidge Farm outlet, something huge began to lumber across the road: a low, round, dark creature walking sweetly, serenely, ever so slowly toward a roadside barbershop. The turtle was so immense, with a shell easily four feet around, that it seemed it must be transplanted from a more exotic habitat—from a place like the Galápagos. Worried at what a highway, and a trip to the barbershop, could hold for an old reptile, I was even more astounded to discover that our present-day city contained such a being. It walked deliberately, unaware of the dangers on every side, huge and unassimilated, darkly radiant, a tragic-comic amalgam: Mr. Magoo and Oedipus at Colonus. All the cars on that road came to a halt, and all the drivers got out of our cars, and we stared as the creature crawled across the macadam, lumbering like memory out of a mostly unseen quarter.

\|\|\| \|\|\| \|\|\|

"We will never know," one of my neighbors says in his living room, speaking of our predecessors in this watershed, the tribe who called the swampy area Menotomet. For many thousand springs, the Pawtuckeogs migrated east from inland forests to set up their summer camps not far from the clam flats of the river and the swamp terrain that gave them water and waterways, fishes, fowl, and silt-rich land for corn. Professor Karl Teeter is a linguistic anthropologist who has spent his life studying the Algonquian family of languages, to which the local tongue, Massachusett, belonged. No living speakers of Massachusett survive, he is saying now, but the language is similar to that spoken by the Maliseet-Passamaquoddy of Nova Scotia. See how the word for "my friend," *neetomp* in Massachusett, is close to the Maliseet *nitap*. But when I press my learned neighbor for native names for the swamp, he has to say, "Place-names are the hardest to recover, and the landscape has changed so much now that I cannot even speculate." We sit for a while turning the pages of the large green book that holds their vocabulary. Karl says some words, and I pronounce them after him: *kushka* (it is wide), *(nu)keteahoum* (we cured him), *kohchukkoonnog* (great snows).

As the native culture reeled, the swampland lay shimmery and resistant to the colonizing touch for another century. European settlers were revolted by the miasmic terrain, and their disdain turned it into a kind of a natural ally for the cause of independence. It was in the soggy outskirts of the Newtowne settlement that patriots could meet and openly plot their revolution. And yet, as soon as technology permitted, the new Americans began to eliminate the wetlands. Orchards first, then a single road through the marshes—the "lonely road," one man called it, "with a double row of pollard willows causewayed above the bog." Just before it began to disappear in earnest, the swamp found its poet in an awkward boy who grew into one of America's finest field ornithologists and taught himself to write a liquid prose:

> When there was a moon, we often struck directly across the open fields, skirting the marshy spots. . . . Invisible and for the most part nameless creatures, moving among the half-submerged reeds close by the boat, or in the grass or leaves on shore, were making all manner of mysterious and often uncanny rustling, whispering, murmuring, grating, gurgling and plashing sounds.

In that passage, William Brewster was remembering his boyhood days. But just after the turn of the century, when the wide river that drained the swamp was narrowed and straightened, and began to receive the discharge of a city sewer, Brewster had to write, "Thus has [the Menotomy] become changed from the broad, fair stream . . . to the insignificant and hideous ditch with nameless filth which now befouls the greater part of the swampy region through which it flows."

Only gentleman naturalists like Brewster and others not especially enamored of the industrial adventure sorrowed when a stand of pines and beeches was cut to make way for an abattoir, when offal was released into the swamp. Or when Fresh Pond was surrounded by icehouses and machinery, when the ice was cut in blocks and sailed in sawdust to Calcutta, Martinique, and the Southern plantations (the ice inspiring, it is said, the Mint Julep). Rail lines appeared just before mid-century, and the story goes quickly then: cattleyards, tanneries, carriage factories. After the clay was discovered, acres were soon covered in clay pits, pugging-mills, and the chimneys of kilns baking their small red loaves. The malleable substrate of the swamp was dug up and made into red-brick Boston, while here, in a gamey landscape, brickyard and railroad workers began to build their modest houses on the edge of the sandy plain adjacent to the swamp. Finally, the terrible malarial epidemic of 1904 and its many small caskets aroused the Commonwealth to civil engineering of a place that was by then commonly referred to as the "menacing lowlands," the area of "nakedness and desolation." Its streams were channeled and sunk in culverts; some of the swamp was dredged and filled to make the site for a tuberculosis sanitarium. Over the next decades, more wetland was filled for pumping stations, suburban subdivisions, and housing projects; for a highway, chemical plants, office parks and playing fields; for a golf course, a gas storage depot and a subway terminal — the last named Alewife, after the blear-eyed herring.

Laying a modern map of our part of the city on Brewster's ink map, I can cobble together an overlay. Where the older map reads "large oaks & Willows" is the site of Porter Chevrolet. Where it says "muskrat pond" is Videosmith. Where it says "heronry of night herons" is Bertucci's Pizza in the Alewife T-Station complex. "Pine swamp" is a grid of two-family houses. Each change was welcomed, was cheered, by the bulk of the population in a country where land seemed unlimited, where swamps were vile and filling them an act of civic heroism.

ꟷꟷꟷ   ꟷꟷꟷ   ꟷꟷꟷ

Once people hear that you are out walking around the neighborhood, nosing into the past, they send you pieces of folded, yellowed paper, copies of photographs and letters. "I'm not a historian," I had to say, "I'm not writing a proper history." But people are generous, and want to make your picture clearer, and want a repository for memory. They bring you the horseshoe they found in their basement. They stand with you in the street, turning the piece of iron over in their hands.

"Yep, a tannery—right where our house stands."

They call you up and tell you about their father, who worked at the rubber factory, their great-uncle from Barbados. At the pizza parlor they say, "This was Lynch's Drugstore. You could get a lime rickey."

At the electrician's office where a neon fist holds a bolt of blue lightning, the polite young electrician who wears Chaps cologne (a lot of it) and is not one bit afraid of electricity but terrified of flying, says, "This was the Sunshine Movie Theatre."

A newspaper clipping comes in the mail: a 1908 headline reads, "Famous Horses Raced Here." And so I came to know the names Flora Temple, Black Hawk, Trustee, the great trotters of their day, and the greatest of them, Lady Suffolk, descended from the legendary Messenger. She pulled her sulky around a race course whose four boundaries have become the four streets that define our enclave. (And under the saddle, she went as fast as a locomotive — a mile in 2:26 minutes — a time so fast that one track reporter gushed it made her name "imperishable.")

My neighbor Joan, a woman who is a candidate for the Society of Those Still Living in the House in Which They Were Born, tells me, "We used to swim in one of the clay pits after it flooded. That was Jerry's Pit. My father sat on the beach barechested and showed his tattoos to the kids. He had an Indian maiden on his shoulder, 'True Love' on his fingers, a goddess jumping rope on his arm, and a navigational star just above his thumb." Another day, over dinner, Joan continues her story: "All of the brickyards but one had closed by the time I was a girl, and there was a lot of trash and white powdery stuff lying around the yards and pits. And some green liquid that never froze. At one place, where the apartment towers are now, the owners put up a sign, 'Clean Fill Wanted,' and one night someone dumped a whole dead horse in the pit. I remember my mother and her friends laughing at that joke until they cried. And I remember the year the city closed our swimming pond down because chemicals had leaked into it. The last clay pit closed in 1952, after it collapsed on a man; it swallowed him and the whole steamshovel he was operating. And that was the end. Later that pit became the town dump."

\\\\ \\\\ \\\\

By the time I arrived in this watershed, the dump was rolling foothills of ooze and decay, fenders, tires, avocado peels and bones, dunes of newspapers and failed appliances, curling irons, bedsprings — all of the trash hummocks circled by scavenging gulls calling their ocean sounds over an inland rot, portions of which were often smoldering with little fires. There were sometimes human scavengers at the dump, a man or woman in a dark overcoat salvaging a child's highchair or a table—an old tradition in this neighborhood. And then it was a park with fields and wildflowers, and a spiraling, sparkling path made of glassphalt. On a recent Sunday, a croquet match was underway—older couples in traditional whites, younger players in flowered shorts and retro Hush Puppy shoes. Under the wickets is the refuse of four decades, capped and monitored, threaded with pipes that allow the mélange to exhale its methane gases and unknowns.

On planning documents the former great swampland is now called the Alewife Area—a place where a modern land-use opera is raging, a big opera with mercantile princes and women in armor, with public officials, a chorus of citizens, and at least one man who sits in a high window and scans for barred owls through binoculars.

The other day I went to the site of the former muskrat pond to rent *'Round Midnight*—to watch again the scene of the old jazz man at his hotel window in Paris, saying, "You don't just go out and pick a style off a tree one day. The tree is inside—growing naturally." Speaking in a voice so graveled with whisky, age, and disease that you have to run the tape back again to make sure you hear him right, Dale Turner is talking about being inevitable. Inside you, he says, growing naturally. Isn't that always the hope: that the human music, our works and chaos pies, could be as right as rain, as a tree, as a glacier coming, gouging, melting into something great.

A L L U V I A L   F A N

By far the largest feature of the Great Swamp to remain is Fresh Pond itself. For twenty years I have circumnavigated Fresh Pond in all seasons, weathers, and moods—running or walking the serpentine path that winds around the water like the rim around an enormous, slightly melted clock. I have run with various souls: a sly, hedonistic Dalmatian named Gus, who unless deeply exhausted could deconstruct whole dinner parties; Anne, who was shedding weight and the wrong husband; Jim, who joined me on night runs during which we admired how Porter Chevrolet's sign laid streamers of sizzling color over the ink-black sheen of the pond. And recently I walked at the pond with my husband, and heard him use the word "rip-rap," a word that public works *cognoscenti* use to describe the rocks placed along a shore. Hearing Peter use that word, casually, reminds me that he is still something of a public works hound, having started his reporter's career covering a suburban public works department. During those years, he often returned home from the embattled, late-night, all-volunteer board meetings exhausted but enthralled by some exotica of the municipal infrastructure. The word also transports me again to the places Peter arranged to take me during our long courtship: tours of waste-water filter systems for the whey runoff from ice cream factories, state-of-the-art silicon chip factories, the power station at Niagara Falls. At Niagara we were given hardhats to wear, and I was allowed to touch one of the chrome sheaths around a three-story-high steel cylinder turbine generating the power for the northeast corridor. (Talk about romance.)

But most often my companion on these walks at Fresh Pond has been the land, the acres that encircle the pond—deciduous woodlands, a little meadow and swale, a stand of white pines, a bog with yellow-limbed willows. The land and the pond itself, on which ice sheets rumble against the shore in winter and canvasbacks bob for their favorite food, wild celery, in fall.

From time to time I exchange rambles at Fresh Pond for lap swimming, lifting weights, and then lolling in a hot tub. The health club in which these activities are accomplished has a skylight over the pool through which a backstroker can admire moons, and during the day, clouds, pigeons, and falling snow. Handsome palms surround the clear, aqua pool water. After my sauna, a nice young person at the front desk gives me a piece of fresh fruit. Driving away from these rituals, I have but a single thought (if you can call it a thought), namely, "Everything is fine." The effect is testimony to the health club's powers, and bringing any calm into this society can only be good, but the effect of Fresh Pond is both more complex and more salutary.

Circling Fresh Pond in all seasons has immersed me in a nuanced portrait of the year, and the pond's fable of constant change within continuity has voided several slings and arrows of outrageous fortune. Here, there will be a feather on the path, a sprawl of tree limbs after a storm, the arrival of geese, the dart of a sodden creature into the woods, a murder of crows cawing over glare ice. Here, the eye is schooled in the play between diffuse and close, taught to count on surprise, to rely on minute things—a dark red leaf encased in ice—to unlock meaning for the metaphor-loving mind. The patterns of light and shadow, thickets and tangles into which we can see but partially, the unspoken-for patches, the water surface that skates toward the horizon—all these are forms and shapes that offer possibilities for mind, for ways of being.

Technically, however, Fresh Pond is a terminal reservoir and purification plant for the city water supply, and that is why it survives. A greensward at the entrance is named Kingsley Park for a famous Victorian president of the Cambridge Water Board. The Honorable Chester W. Kingsley tells his story of the Fresh Pond water works somewhat wistfully, as a man who loves his work and finds few souls able to appreciate the grandeur of an infrastructure: "I have never before had a chance to inform so many on this subject," he writes, "and never expect another such opportunity." Kingsley was president of the Water Board for fourteen years; during his tenure, in 1888, Fresh Pond was ceded to Cambridge by the Commonwealth, the surrounding land included in order to preserve the purity of the water. "The City," writes Kingsley, "has taken about 170 acres, and removed all buildings therefrom. The pond contains 160 acres, and a fine driveway has been constructed all around its borders, nearly three miles long. With the water area and the land taken, this makes a fine water park of 330 acres. The surroundings of the park are being graded and laid out in an artistic way, beautifying the whole region and making it one of the most attractive places in the suburbs of Boston." He continues, "It will thus be seen that in an abundant supply of excellent water . . . Cambridge presents one of the strongest inducements . . . for any who may be looking for a home where good water and good morals prevail."

A water park. How the phrase conveys the Victorian confidence and expansive gesture of a people for whom civic works embodied the democratic ideals: proper comportments of land and water would invite city dwellers into vital and uplifting pleasures, even moral life. It is not hard to imagine Chester Kingsley, bewhiskered, appearing at civic parades in a Water Board Officer's jacket. (Fitted with clever epaulets from which small fountains of water shoot when a concealed bulb is pressed?) Kingsley's comrades in civic proclamations sound the same pleased, confident note: of one scheme for a riverside esplanade, the Cambridge park commissioner envisions that "launches may run from city to city" that "men [may benefit from] this little breathing-space . . . among beautiful surroundings." It was not only a sweet boosterism that led to these claims. The Victorian planners, guided by Frederick Law Olmsted, had noticed the link between qualities of landscape and human well-being.

Reading the Victorians' plans, their bursting pride and energetic efforts, one cannot but feel a tender spot for these city builders who were helping to finish off the exquisite meadows and wetlands. It is hard to fault them when even today many seem not to have understood that only an astonishing one percent of the earth's water is fresh. As the original wetland filtering system was destroyed, modern water planners turned to extraordinary engineering to deliver safe and plentiful water to the city.

One day last winter I visited Mr. Chip Norton, the Watershed Manager, in his offices on the east side of the pond. The Water Department building is a fine old thing from the twenties with Palladian windows, its lobby a near-museum. The space is untended and empty save for a large yellow map of the reservoir mounted on the wall above a fading, dusty model of same, and a very dead rainforest plant near a peeling radiator. The floor is swaddled in brown linoleum, the walls painted pale pink with aqua trim, the effect one of bleak assurance that not one dime of tax money has been wasted here. From the back of the lobby comes a most extravagant and luxurious sound—the thrilling rush of fast water which spills ceaselessly from three holding basins over aerating tiles.

To be greeted by the roar and rush of water is the most brilliant possible entrance to a water department. In the upstairs rooms, city servants are outfitted with carpets, recessed lighting, and the hum of computers, which is well and good, but one prays that the city will have the sense to keep the aura of faded sanitarium that it has going downstairs, in the lobby. At least if this treasure has to yield to renovation, remove it to the Smithsonian as Calvin Trillin's office was (ratty daybed, unspeakable heaps), when *The New Yorker* moved from one side of 43rd Street to the other.

As I pore over the dizzying engineering and planning reports that Mr. Norton has placed on a table in a small reading nook near the reception area, a woman behind the partition is talking on the telephone about where to get some chicken salad sandwiches for lunch. She recommends Armando's Pizza. Long silence. Next she offers to go to Sage's Market, where, she says, they make a delicious chicken salad. Another long silence. Armando's comes up again; the deliberations continue. From behind the other side of the nook a youngish woman sasses an old walrus of a man who has apparently asked her to do some extra task. She replies that she has much more work to do than he does, and besides she has housework on top of that. "Peg always does your housework, I'm sure," she says tartly. The man agrees, takes the comments in stride, sighs, says that it's going to be that kind of day, and then, after a long awkward silence, that it's time for a cigarette.

Other than these essential bureaucratic activities, the municipal water system seems to work by such devices as: having bought water rights a hundred years ago to sources in outlying suburbs; an underground eight-mile-long pipe; gravity; the chemicals alum and chlorine; testing; sedimentation beds and flocculation chambers; sand and charcoal filtration; monster pumps; holding tanks in Belmont; shut-off valves; and more gravity. Mr. Norton lucidly explained all the workings in front of an enormous, wall-size handpainted map of the twenty-three-square-mile watershed for which he is responsible. Merely to gaze on the territory gives one a feeling of expansiveness and excitement—like that associated with mounting a campaign or planning an adventure meant to prove something. The watershed is twice the size of the city it serves, and the wall map reaches well beyond the city, north to the Middlesex Fells, where Mr. Norton used to work and upon which he looks wistfully, recalling how peaceful life was in that rural outpost. In its scale and precision, the map gives the Water Department ante-chamber the air of a war room, the territories of conquest displayed in crystalline detail. But what makes this map wonderful is that its mission is the peaceful delivery of water for washing babies and boiling potatoes—well, for MIT's little nuclear reactor, too, but mainly for aiding the daily lives of citizens.

Perhaps a woman who considers her bathtub the single most important device in the home, whose favorite work is watering plants, and whose day begins with cups of Darjeeling can be forgiven for looking on Mr. Norton a bit dreamily as he pours forth the story of our city's water. It grieves me to see that his nails are bitten to the quick, and I wonder if the Water Department doesn't want to put in a calming eucalyptus tub or steam room at the filtration plant. Like Mr. Kingsley before him, Mr. Norton's chief responsibility is to protect the water quality within his watershed; at Fresh Pond, every use of the land must, he emphasized, be compatible with this goal. Once, while explaining that Fresh Pond is the only place in the state ("maybe in the *world*, save for the Ganges," his look implied) where dogs are allowed to range freely near a public water supply (thus, swim in and befoul it), the watershed manager let a wry look stroll across his face as he added, "But this is Cambridge." He said this with a complex tone that bodes well for his tenure. As we spoke about the reservoir, I was also impressed by Mr. Norton's crisp analysis of what we can and cannot control. "We cannot," he said, "control the past, or birds, for instance. But we can control dogs."

This seemed as he said it like a gnomic reduction of wisdom, and I felt immediately relieved by the idea that the past can be let go of (as far as us controlling it), and also by the clear, calm way he said it. That's right, I thought, admiringly, the past is over. What's done is done. Later I recalled fiction, Proust and Nabokov, and the fact that modulating our idea of the past alters the present. But I know perfectly well what Mr. Norton means. He means, rightly, that he's got a dealt hand. And he is especially not going to be able to control what happened to his watershed and Fresh Pond during the Pleistocene. It was while sitting quietly at the metal table in the Water Department office, studying a heap of maps and surprisingly passionate master plans, with talk of chicken salad sandwiches in the air, that I suddenly, unexpectedly found myself descending again on the plumbline of time, plummeting far past the Great Swamp and its lost heronries to arrive in an entirely other incarnation of our neighborhood.

One Newton Chute provided the geology for the 1944 surficial geologic map of our area. Glancing back and forth between Chute's map and his report, I slowly grasp that Fresh Pond exists on, and that Peter and I make our home on, what was the eastern slope of a river valley. That is: where now exists the ground on which have variously stood drugstores, dray horses pulling blades, and apples in blossom was once merely a volume of air above an enormous river valley that ran southward from present-day Wilmington to the Charles River (which had not yet come into being).

A rock terrace at about eighty feet below present sea level was the bottom of this deep, broad valley; the valley also held an inner gorge that cut down another ninety feet. The presence of the inner gorge indicates to Chute and his colleagues that "at least one important uplift of the land or lowering of sea level occurred during the formation of the valley."

In part, it may be a recent appointment with my dentist, Dr. Guerrara, in which he filled an unusually deep cavity—first boring it out, then filling it in discrete stages with various substances—that makes me riveted by the geological process by which glaciers filled the deep valley. As you may know, the modern human tooth cavity is filled first by a layer of calcium hydroxide, a liquidy paste like Elmer's glue that hardens quickly on the floor of the prepared cavity; then with a thin, cool varnish, painted on to seal the tuvuals; finally with the silver amalgam (copper, silver, tin, small amounts of mercury) that is tamped in, carved, and burnished. The gorge in one's mouth—for so these minute spaces feel to the tongue lost and horrified in the new cavern—is topped up. This is very like what happened all over New England about twenty thousand years ago, in the Pleistocene.

Chute identifies ten principal events in the centuries-long process by which an old valley was filled with successive layers of till, clay, peat, and gravel—materials pushed, trailed, and extruded by a glacier advancing and retreating over the land, moving south and east in a chthonic grading of the surface. Chute accompanies his glacial geology with a map showing which of these glacial fill events figure on the current surface, and where. With mounting excitement, I locate the area of our street on the map: our home-ground is Outwash 4, the eighth event—a layer of sand and pebble-sized gravel that occurred as a large alluvial fan spread southward over the "rock-flour" clays deposited in the exciting seventh event, the clays that would have such consequences for our neighborhood. A small ridge two blocks away, which we now know as Massachusetts Avenue, is thought to be "too high to be part of the fan" and probably was overlayered by its powerful flowing outwash.

I sit back in the Water Department's chair, nearly faint from the morning's events, and my idea of home rearranges itself once more, assimilating the knowledge that we live not only atop a lost swamp but over a buried river valley and on an alluvial fan. It changes things—everything somehow—to know that during all the years I have yearned for life in a bucolic valley my wish has, if prehistorically, been true. And what shall we make of the news that we dwell on an alluvial fan—of all geological events, the one with the prettiest name. While the fine sandy fan was spreading out, Fresh Pond must have still been entirely occupied by a stagnant ice block, for, as Chute reasons, "if the fan had been deposited after the ice block had melted, the depression occupied by the pond would have been filled."

Even the alluvial fan does not prepare me, though, for the fact that our neighborhood, our city, indeed the Eastern Seaboard from Virginia to Nova Scotia, takes place on a crust of earth that was once the west coast of Africa. The crust is named Avalon, and it arrived when a piece of Gondwana, ancient continent, broke away, swept across the ocean (not the Atlantic yet, but Iapetus), and collided with the old North American continent. Our most local crust came from the part of the earth that is today Morocco (and which shares with the Boston Basin the lumpy-looking rock we call puddingstone). It has been quite a long while since these mighty things took place, and it is hard to say what, if anything, they have to do with the *Realpolitik* taking place on the underlying Avalon. But, as always, the familiar when closely observed reveals itself as an exotic.

Beyond its transforming information, a U.S. Geological Survey report enthralls because of the language scientists use to convey glacial events: here there are "geophysical raverses," "thrust faults in overridden sand," "uplift of the land," and "marine embayments." The souls who spin off these phrases in longish sentences that describe — calmly — seismic events that rumbled over millennia, sound as if they know what they are talking about, as if they know what is going on under there down deep, at the level of *accurate subsurface information* where knowledge is grounded.

Although I was born decades after early twentieth-century physicists had their near-nervous breakdowns at the implications of relativity, the fluid epistemology implied has come only slowly and imperfectly into my psyche, which seems to cling to a pre-modern, limbic hope for solidity. As my life's education has proceeded, each new knowledge gradually reveals that it too rests on gossamer metaphor. Reading the geologists, I feel the tantalizing hope that with this vocabulary I might grasp the real nature of things. Perhaps here are the minds and ways of talking that take one through loose gravel, till and sand, through bands of clay, to bedrock. And if it all be gossamer, what better gossamer than bedrock?

NAVIGABLE

One afternoon, circumnavigating Fresh Pond with a xerox of an eighteenth-century map in hand, I see that our local pond was once linked by a series of rivers to the Atlantic Ocean, that for all but the last hundred years of its existence our inland region had a direct channel to the sea. On the old map, the river Menotomy rises out of Fresh Pond, winds through the Great Swamp, joins with the Little River and flows into the Mystic, which empties into the Atlantic. I also see that some vestige of that former water route would still be navigable by canoe. The Little River is extant, and flows into a stream called Alewife Brook, which was formerly the last stretch of the Menotomy. A present-day river guidebook tersely describes Alewife Brook as "not recommended," but Peter and I cannot resist taking a canoe down the pungent, olive-brown stream. As we float past half-submerged shopping carts and debris, we will be moving along the oldest artery of our watershed.

The route will take us through a lock at the Amelia Earhart Dam on the Mystic River, and Peter says, "I think we should get an air-horn to signal the lock keeper." "Great," I said, because I have learned that Peter is always right about gear. There was the time with the Maglite, the incident with the duct tape, the super glue, the extra bike tire, even the three illegal boxes of Happy Lamp fireworks. Many times I have owed my happiness—and once my life—to Peter's gear and his skill with it. So my husband selected an airhorn at the sporting goods store and together we read the instructions, which were very explicit, saying in essence: Do Not Ever Use Your New Air Horn. It Will Destroy Your Ear Drums, So Just Do Not Use This Device Under Any Conditions.

"Oh, they have to say that," Peter said, hefting the little horn. "Some rude people take them to sporting events."

The only other special thing we will need for this journey is an idea about where to land a canoe in a big-city working harbor. The canoe is seventeen feet of a dull green material called Royalex, a stable boat with a low-slung profile, named in honor of the Victorian traveler Mary Kingsley, who liked to paddle in African swamps. We want to land the *Mary Kingsley* somewhere along the banks of the inner harbor, near the Tobin Bridge. On the early summer evening that Peter and I prowl the harbor, we discover not a single take-out site for a canoe, but many other supremely interesting things, including the marine shipping terminal, the titanic legs of the Tobin Bridge, a burned-out pier, the U.S. Gypsum Company, and a mountain of road salt offloaded from an Asian freighter. Near sundown, an oblique red light slants over pools of steamy gypsum tailings. This extravagant light and the sheer muscle of the place make for a seriously romantic landscape, and for romanticism's dark undertow, there is the pier off which things can be tossed. As is often the case, Mr. Emerson has been this way before, admiring the potentially fine face of industry:

> It is vain that we look for genius to reiterate its miracles in the old arts; it is its instinct to find beauty and holiness in new and necessary facts, in the field and road-side, in the shop and mill. Proceeding from a religious heart it will raise to a divine use the railroad, the insurance office, the joint-stock company; our law, our primary assemblies, our commerce, the galvanic battery, the electric jar, the prism, and the chemist's retort . . . The boat at St. Petersburg, which plies along the Lena by magnetism, needs little to make it sublime.

On the other side of the river lies the city of Chelsea, nearly all galvanic battery, a welter of scrap metal yards, weigh stations, warehouses, sugar refineries, gas yards—the last a sinuous complex of pastel pipes almost equal in convolution to that wonder of nature, a Jamesian sentence. As night comes, and a hazy fog begins to materialize, we happen on the Evergood Meat Packing Company, where beams of light from mercury vapor arc lamps rain down on a parking lot, carving the lot out of the night and lighting up this scene: three meat packers in long white butchers' coats, the men running through the lot passing a soccer ball back and forth expertly. The ball bounces from a corrugated wall, skims under the axles of a fleet of trucks. The long white coats are brilliant in the vapor arc light, the fabric flowing, flapping like the wings of birds, like angels, ghosts—like meat packers. It is the quickest glimpse, and now the road climbs a dark hill. From the summit, the city's financial district is visible across the river, its lights flickering, cleaning crews at work. Down the hill, on the river itself, and moored to the bank, lies the object of our search: a small pavilion and public dock.

〣〣〣 〣〣〣 〣〣〣

The most succinct account of our river journey is that we launched a canoe amongst somnolent lily pads and took it out near a Brazilian cargo tanker. The trip begins on the Little River, where, passing the mouth of a narrow, brown ditch full of appliances and engine parts, tin cans, a sodden teddy bear, we are passing the paltry remains of the wide Menotomy. Along one stretch, the Little River is so shallow that it is more a skim-coat of water than a channel, and here the dorsal spines of carp crest the waterline, giving the river the appearance of being alive with silver grey snakes. (See "The Rime of the Ancient Mariner.")

As it deepens again, the Little River becomes Alewife Brook, and when we pass the gas station near Meineke Muffler, we are at the old site of a basketry weir, a spot that both native Americans and settlers used for harvesting shad and alewives—the latter plentiful still enough in the nineteenth century to move one observer to write, "I have seen two or three hundred taken at a single cast of a small seine." Up to the present day, new citizens come to this watershed in spring to catch alewives. On another day at the Mystic Dam, we meet three delicate Cambodian men whose fishing gear consists of a box of large pink garbage bags. The men are barefoot, wearing dated bell-bottoms and white dress shirts (vintage Goodwill), and they fish from slippery rocks, dipping the pink plastic bags into the causeway spill. Although the numbers of the fish are greatly diminished, at this dam in spring they can look abundant, flowing over the spill into the plastic bags like grains of rice from a bulk bin—that thick and fast. The bargain-brand bags that the men wield are so thin that the fishes deform the poly, stretching it until eyes, fins, and tails are visible through the petroleum pink.

An alewife is an *anadromous* fish ("running upward"), and its presence in our watershed is known as *ephemeral*. The fishes are seasonal transients, coming from the ocean to freshwater to spawn. Continuing south now on the Mystic River, we are following the young alewives' fall route back to sea. They would pass, as we do now, backyard barbeques and hammocks, and then the backside of a downtown, where retaining walls read "Sally luvs Rick," "Just Say Yes," and "Dragons Rule," where a crumbling infrastructure crawls with organic patterns, subtle grays and browns, white encrustations—a spectacular topography whose decay and struggle engage the eye, which recognizing its own condition, sympathizes.

Here and there, trees overhang the river, dappling its surface of lily pads and oily gloves. As the river widens the treebreak disappears. We pass by an Edison power plant, and under a bridge that bears eight lanes of interstate traffic. The Amelia Earhart Dam comes into view. Peter readies the airhorn, and when the dam is close, he presses the small button. It delivers one of the loudest sounds I have ever heard—next to the time a lightning bolt hit the house and made me wonder, for a second, if I had been shot. The lock keeper likes the airhorn, likes being hailed in the proper nautical way, and gives Peter a crisp salute. As *Mary Kingsley* glides into the narrow chamber, two powerboats hurry in behind us. The doors of the lock slide closed, the water rises, and when the lock opens again, the still, olive river water has vanished and we are in an ocean-blue chop with whitecaps.

The powerboats take off like rodeo cowboys on broncos, and I am wishing that we had something to rev too, some throttle to gun. As the wind picks up, first tugboats, then small freighters appear. Conveyor belts, rigs, and tall booms are cantilevered over the water; a grand silver dome built to cover twenty tons of unrefined sugar glints on the bank. By the time the big bridge looms into view, our canoe has shrunk to a bobbin—a bit of flotsam far below the gantry cranes. We are gawking at the cranes like rubes on Broadway when a rogue ocean swell rises out of nowhere, tosses the canoe four feet into the air, spins us a little, breaks across the side, slaps us full-face with salty water. The pavilion and dock are just visible now on the other side of the river, and as we struggle toward the landing in the chop, we marvel at the people who took their thinner, lighter canoes out much farther, into open ocean, and up and down the Atlantic coast.

At the dock we are met by two small boys, brothers, who shyly stare and beam at the canoe, and within seconds of our invitation are in it, are touching its sides, are gripping the paddles, are putting on lifejackets, are not sitting too still but gently rocking the boat to get a feel for it. Their names, the boys tell us, are Ulysses and Erik.

I wouldn't dream of making that up, and where else but a big-city waterfront would you expect, these days, to be met by the two chief heroes of epic seafaring? True to their names, the boys cannot take their eyes off our boat. They are intrigued by paddles. Fascinated by the weight and color of life jackets. Overjoyed by ropes, by tying knots. Desirous to know what the canoe is made of. Running their hands over the cane seats and wooden thwarts. In love with all things nautical. Beside themselves with happiness when their father says, yes, they can take a short ride with us, just around the perimeter of the dock, not far. And when at last we must head home, the legends (as gallant, as bold, as clever as ever) cajole us, insist on hauling some of the gear up the slight incline to our waiting car, where they are further enthralled by the every detail of mounting a canoe on a Subaru coupe: how the canoe is lifted up by two people, how it is strapped onto the roof of the car, how foam clips are slipped over the gunnels, how ropes are laced and tightened.

Ulysses and Erik tell us that they were born here, in this city, but that home is an island far from here, somewhere over the water. They each point out to sea, not exactly in the same direction. When the canoe has been secured in place, and all the gear stowed, the hero-boys shimmer away, are last seen lying flat on their stomachs, their arms submerged in water up to the shoulderblades—as close to being in the ocean as boys on dry land can be.

ERRAND

\\\\\\   \\\\\\   \\\\\\   \\\\\\

The moon and sun are eternal travelers. Even the years
wander on. A lifetime adrift in a boat, or in old age leading a
tired horse into the years, every day is a journey.
> —Matsuo Bashō, *Narrow Road to the Interior*

WHAT A COMFORT words can be—stays, pitons on a
cliff—and each is also a house of history and a slippery fish. "Errand" has been roughly treated, a word whose many meanings have
narrowed to just one: a short journey to perform some simple task
of life. Often an employee or a child is sent to perform the task, but
no longer is the sent soul known as an errand-bearer. No one uses
errand-carts, or goes on those "errands into the wilderness" the Puritans so liked. Moderns do still go on fool's errands, although never
on "sleeveless" ones—or rather, persons *do* go on those errands
leading to nothing (being sent by Pope Alexander to convert the
Sultan of Iconium was one), but do not have so fine a name for
them. And who calls anymore on the embassies and expeditions of
"Immortal forms, / On gracious errands bent," the comings and go-
ings of Hierarchies and Thrones, those beings who can roam earth
and underworlds with their messages, or send an errand to heaven,
as they please.

‖‖‖ ‖‖‖ ‖‖‖

Many of my errands are performed along a broad avenue a few blocks east of our house. The post office is there and a family-run market famous for its fruit baskets wrapped in colored cellophane. There is a stationer, the kind whose shelves hold the wild promise of blank paper and new pens, and simultaneously embody an old idea of order: envelopes and rubber bands stacked by size, tubes of oil paint nestled in boat-like slots, each color with a berth. There is a consignment shop so chock-full of teacups and porcelain that even a small woman can feel like a bull. The Socrates Newtowne Grille is on the avenue, also a boutique named Dish, a Turkish café, and a laundry (land of Steve, zen master of folding). It is a midwinter afternoon, and I am on a round of errands along this avenue near the very edge of a city. It has been snowing for nearly a week.

The only problem with life on the edge, of course, is the edginess of it, but at the latest café to open on the doomed corner along this stretch, someone has stuck a glossy sticker on the window, a black-and-pink number that reads, "IF YOU'RE NOT LIVING ON THE EDGE, YOU'RE TAKING UP TOO MUCH SPACE." A declaration like that is a sign, from whom we do not know, but it suggests enough souls on the edge to support the cost of a silk-screen run.

‖‖‖ ‖‖‖ ‖‖‖

The post office has a foyer, one wall made entirely of P.O. boxes with brass doors and glass windows. In the main room, a sleek philatelic display revolves silently near an exhibit of three mailing cartons, prices scrawled on the sides. There are no other

customers as I walk in, but the clerks like you to observe the handwritten sign: "Wait here until called." I wait with a parcel in my
arms and two letters with the new Coleman Hawkins stamp on
them. For as long as I can remember, I have adored sending and re-
ceiving mail, selecting commemorative stamps, and anticipating
what a Monarch or No. 10 envelope may hold—and thus I adore
the post office, too, in the way that a woman who loves to cook de-
lights to honor and respect her pots and pans. She is interested in
their condition and upkeep, the accoutrement of their being, because they are central to an outcome upon which she relies for happiness.

"Next," says the clerk. I'll call him Lyle.

"Hi, Lyle. What's that under your lip?"

"It's sort of an experiment; they call it a jazz dot. First class? Any
books inside?"

"It's not a jazz dot, it's a soul patch," the other clerk yells from the
sorting room. "I have to tell you *everything*."

Lyle ignores Bobby.

"Yes. No books. What do you mean by an experiment, Lyle?"

"He's in love," Bobby says, passing the counter.

"This is three dollars," Lyle says to me. "Anything else?"

"What are your commemoratives today?"

Lyle pulls out the drawer of stamps for me to look, and turning to
his tormentor, announces, "This. Is. A. United. States. Post. Office."—pronouncing each word distinctly, invoking all the propriety of the great office whose appointed rounds are not stayed by rain
nor sleet nor snow; whose "ceaseless labors pervade every . . . theatre of human enterprise"; which "mingles with the throbbings of
almost every heart in the land"; the service that is "the delicate ear
trump through which alike nations and families and isolated indi-

viduals whisper their joys and their sorrows, their convictions and their sympathies, to all who listen for their coming."

"I'm bad, I'm *bad*," Bobby says.

Lyle turns back to me, fully recovered.

"Do you need a receipt? They're free today."

On this winter day the two clerks are wearing gray cardigans, but in summer they may wear gray Bermuda shorts, the hardy getup of field biologists and intrepid explorers. I say that a group of (still mostly) guys who show their legs deserve our approval in an era when businessmen are persuaded that extra-long socks are *de rigeur* to prevent sightings of (gasp!) flesh during executive leg-crossings. As I leave the P.O., a barely recognizable version of "Georgia on My Mind" is playing in the background—a perfect music to send mail on its journey toward motorized carts, elevators wired for crooners, the cold bellies of jets.

||| ||| |||

Where the snow has been shoveled and scraped away, the mica-rich sidewalk glitters like democracy. A vent of steam ghosts from a manhole; a snow devil whirls off the top of a bank, filling the air with a small spangled tornado; a cupful of sun spills over the rim of a woolly cloud. A gleaming epic coming at you gratis can make you feel like you're getting away with something, although its story may be hard to follow and any one of these things is an infinite who-dunit: the mica in the cement; the two monks passing; the steam coming out of the tall industrial mouths, white snakes rising, shedding smoky skins into the winter air; the blood-red flags on the roof of the hamburger place bright and rippling with a greed now so interwoven in this land with grace that greed and grace are like the single indivisible heart of Siamese twins.

‖‖ ‖‖ ‖‖

Smack next to the P.O., in the same 1920s sandstone building, is a sporting goods and gun shop, a deer head mounted in the
window above a collection of wildlife T-shirts. Inside, the smell
that rises from the old wooden floorboards is a Proustian cookie for
anyone who was a child in small town with a hardware store, or a
five & dime (the kind with a Maybelline counter, and glass dividers
corralling handkerchiefs and bobby pins).

The goods of the gun and sports store are arranged roughly in order of lethality. The front shelves hold bandannas and wicker picnic hampers with aqua plates, evoking an outdoor pastoral which
gives way in the middle section to shelves of ointments that make a
man smell like a female deer, and boxes of thermal gloves, toe-
heaters, and a wall of fishing lures: Jig-in-a-Tube, the Slug-Go, and
Mister Twister; the Do-Sump'n lure with flame-colored tentacles;
a shelf of Pork Crawdads; a fish scale called the De-Liar. The lures
gradually feather into a shelf of game-callers—Bleat Deer, Goose
Flute—and boxes of bulk bullets shrink-wrapped in bronze plastic.
By the bullets there is a clothesline hung with canvas hunting suits,
the fabric printed with a realistic bark pattern. (Shades of *Mac-
beth*—the body as the moving wood.) The threshold to the back
room, the gun room, is marked by a moose head mounted high
near the ceiling on a supporting column. Here in the city it is easy
to forget how big a moose is—this head is larger than a steamer
trunk. It is large enough to preside, with glass eyes, a cracked nose,
a still silky chestnut-brown neck.

A block from the moose and down one flight of stairs is the
copy shop run by Art, a room with three large machines that exude
the hot electrical smell of warm plastic. Art is an even-tempered

man with dark blue eyes. "Ocean-blue," he says. He's right. He wears black jeans, black boots, workshirts. Assistants come and go in the shop, several each year, but Art is constant, has managed the place for ten years. In his room one flight underground, Art copies tax forms, sheet music, resumes, manuscripts, and bake sale flyers. He prints up business cards and wedding announcements. He can make a sign for a new tailor or a bakery. In the second year of our acquaintance, Art began to fling me the key to the self-service machine, bypassing the need for a change purse of quarters and nickels. "Just tell me the number," he said.

Today his counter is solid customer, each one with an urgent request—a birth announcement, a dissertation, a petition. Six days of the week, Art takes the wall of urgency that arrives in his room and melts it by his evenness, his patience. Everyone's copies get done, and they are done well or else they're done over, and people leave saying "Thanks, Art." While the manager dissolves the present line of impatience, I wait by the bulletin board, reading the sheaf of notices pinned to the cork: saxophone lessons, grief counseling, a Tercel for the best offer.

Do we mix the pigment of days with the binder of our bodies? Carrying water to plants in the morning, I could be a raincloud, something that does not ask why it exists. I fill up a jug and pour the water; the water sinks into the soil, sometimes making a sighing sound as the earth absorbs the liquid. The water disappears; a humid smell fills the air. The leaves are beaded. What is that wish to be the gray-green of the leaf, to be like water soaking in? In a society compulsive about production, is it an art to subside, to cease, to sink? Naturally, everything happens in a specific gravity, and passing through the sieve of a culture's toxins must be one of the essential finings. But can a lifework happen in unrecorded moments, be something the self does unawares? By definition, this cannot be a commodity and it would be almost invisible. How could this good, whatever it is, be coaxed from hiding, from latency? When the rush is over and Art is free, I pick up a paper clip.

"I've been thinking," Art blurts.

"Uh-oh."

"I've been thinking about going," Art says.

"Going?"

"Heading out," Art elaborates.

"Do you mean leave the store?"

"The store, the country. I'm thinking of heading out."

"Where would you head?"

"I'm thinking about Spain," Art says. "Maybe Ireland, the South Pacific. I've got friends on St. John's. Russia, Madagascar . . ."

Art names most of the known world. "Machu Picchu, Japan . . ."

I nod.

"I'd have to close the shop, of course."

"Of course."

Art is speaking in truncated phrases, nearly gasping for breath.

"Save my money for about a year. . . . I've been . . . saving . . . for a while. . . . And then go . . . for . . . I'm thinking . . . about a year."

Abruptly Art stops his tour of the globe and spreads his hands in the air, like a prosecutor resting, the scope and breadth of his case completely aired. He bends down to hunt for a ream of paper in a cubbyhole and asks in a muffled voice, "Is this a good idea?"

Many people will be glad when Art returns from traveling. Here, where his machines pulse with flashes of light, the man is admired. Here he has made one of the ephemeral communities of a city, gathering citizens as easily as a knife-grinder at his wheel collected an earlier metropolis. (With a light but firm hand, said Whitman, the knife-grinder held his blade to the stone, and there issued forth then "copious golden jets, Sparkles from the wheel" — the incidental beauty of the modern city.) We're into Fodor's guides when a new customer floats down the stairs and unfurls a child's finger-painting: a house with a turtle landing on the roof.

"These will be ready tomorrow morning," Art says of my stack, and I go on down the avenue toward the shopping center, an open-air relic from the fifties. Who can lament the enormity of choice; it is the premise of the land, and we are spores of an immense bloom that long ago burst. But for every Vietnamese girl who arrives and becomes a surgeon—a lovely one was on the news the other night, pure grit unbuckled from a scripted past—there must be millions who falter in chance. Passing the cleaners, I see Mrs. N-, sorting a heap of shirts. Behind her, the overhead belt carries dresses and slacks, swishing in their plastic tunics, swooping along an undulating track suspended from the ceiling. A few weeks ago I brought in my husband's black kimono. It has two white emblems above the breast, and on the inside, modestly, a riverside village woven in grey-green silks: two women fishing, two ducks, a dumpling seller near the bridge, a boat being poled through a ripple. Together, Mrs. N- and I stuck small red adhesive arrows on the stained places, and she noticed a rip forming in the seam of one sleeve.

"Tuesday—okay?"

Rounding the corner into the mall, a teenager with a hood pulled low looks surprised when our eyes meet, then grins. A look can pass between strangers, kin to the look countrymen may give finding one another in a far place. My, my; you as you, me as me. The recognition goes so unremarked as not to exist in any official account. It has taken me most of my life even to notice the look, which happens, I suppose, in the interstices of everyone's life.

The windows of the shopping center are full of reflective red foil hearts and cupids flying with champagne glasses in hand, and in the sky over the lot the hunger moon of January is rising huge and unobstructed, orange-red through the city's exhalation of gases. We live in an unintended landscape of still-damp, coexisting scriptures. Coming home once from the north, I crested the glacial hills and the city popped up, as it always does, as though a hand has pulled a cord. I was aware, that morning, of the many ways that love can go wrong and I might have faltered again, but coming down the long hill into the basin and seeing the city, the hive inventing itself, storing and translating generations, one for another, I felt a slight stirring, a coalescence, like a few grains of sand lodging in the lee of some dried grass. That was the way courage came to me, just enough to cantilever love, to transfer its improbable spirals and towers to a ground.

"Buy a copy of *Spare Change*," sing-songs the man at the entrance to the Star Market. "Help the homeless, get your *Spare Change* fresh and hot off the press."

His high, clear intonation recalls the Dublin street song that we learned as children, "Cockles and mussels / alive, alive-o." The cold of the cobbled streets, and the salt and clink of black-blue shells of mussels, which we had not yet touched, had descended through a century, crossed an ocean, come into the fluorescent room of an elementary school. How does a song do that?

"Love your hat," the man says as he takes a dollar for the paper.

Are things truer if said aloud? Inside the market there is a "two-for-one" roasting-chicken special. Two chickens suggest a future. Maybe to have lived at all is the thing. I buy the chickens, and a melon, and a box of After Eight mints, which an elegant man I know likes, and when I put the box in the wire cart, the man's confident manner hovers briefly above it. I hold on to the cart. At the end of the soft drink aisle, a woman is handing out samples of a dill-flavored hummus spread. She spreads puréed chickpeas on crackers, sets the samples on small white paper plates. The woman is in her late sixties, dressed in a good wool skirt and a pale yellow sweater set, and she has the air of someone just up from a nap, features still settling into a face. I wish I could hug her. She has a certain line to say: "If you'll try a carton of Mr. Hummus today, you'll also get . . . ," but she speaks so softly it's hard to tell what the free thing is. You can see that she is surprised at the whole idea of herself proposing a dip. To strangers. She's trying. Is the family like a mobile, a floating thing that shivers and moves when any one of its pieces is touched?

Outside the sky has turned a slatey, indigo blue, one of the blues that is the scattering of dust in air. Carrying the two chickens and the Mr. Hummus, I go north now along the avenue, passing the Maharaja restaurant and the window treatment place with Mohawk blinds.

The cold and gray-blue light recall another Art, the one made up by Madame Estella in Atlantic City. That was a winter day like this one, in late January, when two other painters and I had fled school for a day. The landscape painter had a car and she knew of a palm-reading place on the boardwalk. It would be open, she promised. This was a winter in the lull between the floy-floy years and Caesar's Palace, when the boardwalk scene was waddling seagulls. Madame Estella, with very black hair and a fuzzy car-coat, told the future in a room as small as an ice-fishing hut but swagged in scarves and patchouli incense, and lit by a flotilla of votive candles in red shot glasses.

My friends went first. Out the window, the ocean and sky were the same gray, the water distinguished from air only by its metallic sheen. I didn't know then how to account for the future, except to imagine that it must have some root in the present, and that the present might be formed like clay on a wheel, with attention to the amount of air kneaded into a slab, the amount of water from the elephant-ear sponge, the speed of the wheel, and the gesture that arose in the hands and telegraphed to the spinning slip. The future might be touchable in that way. But Madame was speaking of another future, shown in the movements of planets, each of which had its own house. Which was nice. She placed my palm in her own, ran her index finger along a "life line" and a "heart line."

The life line, she said, was broken. I saw that she was right; it was a skein of bundled strands. At first she said it wouldn't be a long life, then that it would be long enough but would stop and start again. Looking at my palm in Estella's hand was looking down on a moist topography flecked with paint, and one dark purple spot in the mound beneath the thumb—the remains of a thorn which you could see under the skin like the tip of a branch under ice. The Atlantic giantess rocked beneath the shack, and it felt nice to have my hand held by a woman with a fake name and dyed hair. Madame spoke for ten minutes, during which time she made no comment about my future as a painter, the subject then uppermost in my mind. So when the reading was over, I asked, "May I ask a question?"

"Yes, dear."

"What about art?"

Madame Estella cradled my palm again, studied it, and said, "You will be married in two years!"

I was too polite to laugh, but we did later, outside, and again when we passed the roadside elephant at Margate, cousin to the three-story ear of corn, the immense fiberglass fish, the giant sombrero motel. The creature had a gazebo for a saddle, and massive legs planted in hard-pack sand, legs which were not in correct proportion to the body. They were like a basset hound's, short and squat. But we could easily sympathize with the designers; it must have been hard to engineer any legs at all for a colossus. This one was large enough to have a staircase inside its legs and belly. Maybe you went up into the head, looked out through large eyes to the sea.

By the time the weird sister turned out to be right about life stopping and starting again, I knew enough to know you can hardly go wrong with that prediction. You look, you see it all the time. It's starting again now as the city goes home in the snow, each bundled pedestrian a receding swirl, like the wintry figures of Utrillo's Montmarte. And again as snowbanks receive their shadows, as spray paint propagates on the Greek restaurant wall, as the cook inside pats eggs of rice into grape leaves pulled from brine.

PLOT

IIII   IIII   IIII

THE DAY WAS SO HOT that the pumps at the Merit station were undulating in sheets of octane-scented air, so hot the city looked blanched—the cement sidewalks and canvas awnings pale, and our houses pale in their shingles and jackets of aluminum siding. The attendant gestured with the end of a fuel nozzle, wand of petroleum man. "Yes, ma'am," he said, "right down the block." Young men were just starting to call me ma'am. By the office door, the cola machine pleaded *cool cool* with a big bluish photograph of ice cubes the size of car batteries and a torrent of soda coming over the cubes like a stupendous falls, like a natural wonder.

One block farther, at the end of a sizzling, shadeless street, and I was walking through a prairie of tall, airy cosmos in feathery bloom, through lanes of nodding dahlias, trellised tomatoes, and a stand of tasseled bantam corn. I passed a hybrid tea and a heavy old courtesan of a rose (Souvenir de la Malmaison? Nymph's Thigh?), also patches of opal basil and cayenne, the pepper leaves cloaking slender red fingers. The bees of summer were murmuring by the hour in foxglove bells, exactly as Wordsworth saw them in his praise of the surprising freedom to be found in the sonnet's measured and scanty plot of ground. (They must have been the late-blooming Ambigua, which can stand a little heat.) Everywhere too went white gypsy moths, a bane as infants but harmless now. The squash vines were sticky, and—it was not a mirage—something was stirring in the green: a woman, wearing a proper urban gardener's outfit of black mini-skirt, tank top, high heels.

At last count, there are twelve community gardens in our city. The one I am describing, where I have planted for ten years, lies squarely in the floodplain of a once-muscular river, a block from three gas stations and two highways. The land is divided into about sixty twelve-by-twelve-foot plots, which are assigned to citizen gardeners for an annual fee of five dollars. Over the years I have watched many other passersby respond to this quarter acre: women in suits and running shoes who let themselves lean for restful minutes on the fence, a bent man with a walker who makes the perimeter of the garden the path of his constitutional, children who begin their spontaneous dances.

There are many differences, of course, between a private and a communal garden, but in one respect they are the same. Often I want only to get out in the dirt, to tamp down some shell bean seeds—the kidney-shaped Jacob's Cattle, white with maroon blotches like an Appaloosa pony, is nice—or pull weeds, or give the place a little water. But that is not the way with gardens. Whatever kind of garden one has, the seeds *mean*, the weeds *mean*, the watering and the tamping down *mean*. It all seethes with meaning—"imaginary gardens with real toads in them," said Marianne Moore, and she wasn't kidding.

One of the chief meanings of the community garden is suggested by the landscape architect Clare Cooper Marcus, who describes a study of a hundred suburban gardens in the San Francisco

Bay area. The study revealed that the gardeners were less interested in discovering which plants were suited, ecologically speaking, to their locale, its climate, and soil, than in growing plants that gave them the feeling of being *at home.* Thus: "A man from Oregon wanted roses, gladioli, and a blue spruce. A woman of Italian descent planted the same vegetables her mother had grown. . . . A teenaged girl, who loved 'Hawaii Five-O,' created a tropical jungle."

That is precisely what goes on in our community garden, except that rather than being dispersed over the greater reaches of suburbia, here all the notions of home are packed together, closely, in the pluralistic intensity of a modern city. Each of the plots of this big garden is cultivated by a different person, and true to the radical premise of America, each plot proposes an individual notion of what a garden *is.* What it should look like. What should grow in it. And why. And how much. And with what techniques and substances, following what principles, rites, or calendar. (That is: aesthetics, ethics, philosophy, technology, economy, ecology, and religion.) Stroll down any of the criss-crossing paths and you will come upon as many ideas of order and beauty, as many ideas of a proper agriculture, and as many ideas about how to support the lank vines of indeterminate tomatoes as there are plots.

To a European garden designer like Capability Brown (so called because he so often spoke of the "capability" of the estates in his charge), the resulting mélange would probably not be considered a garden at all, but only a desultory new world compost heap. But to an American eye, a field composed of many squares easily recalls the patchwork of one of our most indigenous, most specifically American artforms. Entering this particular garden by the side gate, the first idea to meet the eye is a grid of Cartesian rationality, wooden stakes at exact intervals, each stake bearing a Big Boy tomato neatly tied with twine, the ground mulched in silvery salt-marsh hay. Steps from this anthem to plain geometry lies a plot of johnny jump-ups that are allowed to erupt each spring in random patches, an arrangement in sympathy with the new ideas about chaos, which seems to be better for us than we used to think. Next is a sprawl of leggy sweet peas and poppies curling around a seated stone Buddha: the deep impersonal smile, the tapering hand pointing to the heart.

Adjacent to the plot of the Four Noble Truths grow rows of rare and out-of-fashion plants, among them tomatillos that produce papery lantern-like pods. A rumpled young man raises these neglected botanicals, saves the seeds, then mails them around the country to other seed-savers. It is a tender, intelligent activity by which considerable genetic material is kept viable. Why does it make his garden even more winning that the earnest young man so rarely cultivates his rarities that they are always mixed up with bladderwort, tansy, and lamb's quarters—three of the most common wild plants of our region?

Hard by the rescue mission lies a science project, with transparent plastic cones surrounding each plant, with gauges, with a chart marked with temperatures and fluctuating pH levels. (Our soil is slightly acidic and can always stand a little lime.) The lab director is often accompanied by dates. "You really know how to water," I hear her tell one, a young man who is methodical, who gives the plants more than a cosmetic soaking. I can see his blush two rows away.

And here comes the garden of basil, eggplant, and plum tomatoes—the Mediterranean triumvirate which make up the sauce garden of a woman whose family name is the name of a Sicilian village. Who pressed upon me her grandmother's recipe for put-

tanesca, the sauce of whores. And here is a go-for-broke scheme—
an entire plot filled with runners and leaves funneling life to a single swelling pumpkin that could bring ten thousand dollars in
prize money if the ambitious vegetable lumbers into the nine-
hundred-pound range. The pumpkin is being nurtured by two mu-
sicians; Plan B, they say, in their plan for financial security: aggres-
sive growth. And now we are passing the plot that was long the garden of the late Mrs. Fanny Dinkins, who grew collards—each
dusty, silver-green leaf robust enough to be a roofing tile—and educated me about the sweet potato crops of her South Carolina
homeland: how sweet potatoes are harvested, stacked, and covered
in straw and earth for winter storage, how these mounds rose over
the landscape of her girlhood, how to slip your hand into a mound
and extract enough sweet potatoes for dinner.

Our own garden has held Georgia-brand collards, the beet
called Detroit Dark Red, and a hybrid tomato from Japan, the
Odoriko, whose name, we learn via e-mail from one of Peter's
colleagues in Tokyo, is the most old-fashioned Japanese word
for dancer. The modern word, Hattori-san explains, is *dansaa*,
whereas "Odoriko" connotes an antique, nearly ancient figure,
something close to our "Terpsichore." Recently, after a spring
when we were traveling and could merely throw in a handful of lettuce seeds, we returned (in trepidation) to find our plot awash in
chives, tuffets of velvety pansies, and tall blue cornflowers—one of
our most beautiful gardens, all of it blown to us on the wind.
"You've got my cornflowers," said the woman three gardens down,
laughing at the way wind toys with our ideas of possession.

All the individual ideas of this garden coexist, their ideo-
logical borders somewhat blurred by roving tendrils, by nastur-
tiums flopping over lines, by old onion tops collapsing onto roses,

and by the host of glossy black crickets who easily hop from plot to plot, and theory to theory, like itinerant circuit preachers. Situated in a dense residential zone, close to the slew of gas stations and ceaseless traffic, this especial Acadia is also cheek-by-jowl with a factory that did something smart and important to help win WW II (including making the synthetic rubber bunadrene-styrene), but whose name has since been linked with phrases like "toxic sludge."

Naturally, the soil of a garden located amongst the dregs of an old semi-industrial landscape is suspect. Here, someone re-tests our garden soil every few years, and one year it was me. As a sharp woman at the County Extension Service explains, it is a very rare piece of urban earth that contains no lead or toxic metals such as cadmium or aluminum in its composition. The usual level of lead is about 15 to 40 parts per million parts of soil—on a scale in which 33 parts per million in the sample is low, 110 is high, and anything over 300, the EPA wants children and pregnant women *out of the area*. But the five-page report from the County Extension says our garden soil contains 8 parts per million—incredibly, *lower* than the amount of lead naturally present in most soils.

It may just be one of those confluences that we call luck, which is perhaps a subspecies of grace. We are lucky that any remaining naphthalene sludge leaching from old waste lagoons moves across the watershed in a course that misses our garden. Lucky that during the worst decades of auto lead emissions, our garden land lay blanketed under layers of greenhouse detritus—a modern midden of pot shards, ungerminated bulbs, and surplus plants. We are lucky that since the time of its creation during the last ice age, the land of this garden has remained open. And we are lucky that the land is owned by a man descended from Swedish horticulturists, a man whose family has run the greenhouse business across the road from the garden for nearly a century, filling its long, moist bays with seasonal seas of poinsettias, tulips, lilies, and mums.

One afternoon after weeding, I walked across the street and found Ed sitting at his oak rolltop desk in the greenhouse office. I was wondering about the origin of the garden, guessing that it might have a back-to-land-urban-hippie history.

"No," said Ed, "it started with Jim Royster, who lived up the street." Ed points to a house several doors down. "He was from Georgia, originally, or North Carolina. One day Royster came over to talk about starting a garden on our field. We had used it for mums for many years, but then the labor costs killed us and we let it go. It had gotten wild with witch grass, and to tell you the truth, we pooh-poohed Royster. But Jim was a friendly guy, and he was speaking pie-in-the-sky, and finally we thought, 'This is something special.' And we said yes."

For four decades, the Norbergs had enriched their chrysanthemum land with peat moss and organic matter. And it was good land to begin with—alluvial, washed for centuries in the bottom silt from the Menotomy River. The colonial farmers, who planted this region in the 1800s and called it Watson's Plain, thought the soil was among the best in the Boston Basin. Our present-day garden also lies not far from the summer villages of the first people of this region, who supplemented their diet of fish and clams with beans and corn. The women of the tribe were the planters, and moderns who study their agricultural technique consider it rather good: the beans fixed nitrogen, the corn husks which the women left to decay restored nutrients to the soil, erosion was minimal, and yields were high. One day, while I was weeding a patch of peppery Rocket aru-

gula, these several facts about tribes, terrain, and time floated together into one of the synapse junctions of mind, and I understood
that my garden neighbors and I are cultivating our Earligolds,
Gladiators, Spacemasters, Silver Queens, and Florida Giants on
land that women may have planted for—a conservative guess—
seven thousand years.

But the atavism of the modern gardener does not require so
very ancient a regression. I am hardly unusual in having, on both
sides of my family and for hundreds of years, ancestors who were
principally farmers. There is a fifteenth-century court messenger
on my father's family tree, and here and there appears a minister,
blacksmith, or scribe, but I am only the third generation in my family's history not to derive my principal livelihood from the earth.
Surely it is not hard to understand why we feel an inscape of affection for the anchorage and nutrient reservoir called soil, savoring its moist texture in our hands, the feel of its crumbling tilth.
Surely it is no mystery why we also like plants, like to touch and admire them, give them all they want, and later, prance around the
kitchen (or the state fair) with a bunch of purple-top turnips,
mound them up like sumptuous Flemish still-lifes, tie blue ribbons
to their stalks.

However much one has the gene for "Grow too many vegetables
and give a lot of them away and put some of them up for winter,"
the urban pastoral now unfolding on this field operates, like the city
in which it occurs, with the good manners of urban distance—the
manners that allow for fizzy encounters and easy retreats from
same. Thus the community in community garden is a loose alliance, and for all the goods that one garden produces—tomatoes
with real flavor, cutting flowers, connections, calmer minds—it is

no covenant of survival like the gardens of yore. (A Star supermarket, a White Hen Pantry, an Asian grocery, and a Bread & Circus are right down the street.) I know of other gardens in this city that have changed whole neighborhoods, and of a prison garden where a man says, "These green things made me feel like a human being again." This garden did not have so much healing work to do, but the land was once a field of rubble and now it is not, and survival takes many forms: it is no small thing for urban people to touch the earth, to know when the moon will be gibbous, when to expect the last frost, to nod to perfect strangers, get to know some of them, sing out "Want me to leave the water on for you?" Though we make no formal propitiations to this land, like our predecessors surely did, we are all grateful for it, and we do have one crucial ritual — as important for our crofts as the long days of sun and soaking rains.

The Annual Meeting convenes on a Saturday morning at ten o'clock in early March, when the ground of New England is still frozen and often sealed by a deep dream of snow. Lately we have begun to meet in the basement of a concrete-block building constructed a hundred years ago by Jamaican immigrants as a house of worship. Empty for several decades in the early twentieth century, the church was for a long time a custom woodworker's shop, and recently it has come nearly full circle:

"*Bienvenue, je vous en pris,*" says the sexton, as we enter the warm basement meeting room of what is now an *église Hatien.*

The longtime coordinator of our garden community calls the meeting to order. Bill is a soft-spoken, plain-spoken man who wears blue jeans, a clean white shirt, and black sneakers. He is the picture of a man with his feet on the ground, so it is a surprise to learn that he spends most of his time contemplating, if not actually in, the thermosphere—which, as you may know, is that part of the atmosphere between the mesopause and the height at which the earth's atmosphere ceases to have the properties of a continuous medium. It's an exotic little sphere, way way up there. Bill's work is modeling the behavior of communication signals in the thermosphere, behavior that is, to summarize Bill's account, "highly unpredictable."

For almost eight years, Bill has been the ideal leader of our neofeudal garden world, the kind of leader that Lao Tsu admires in the *Tao Te Ching*, a leader so good that he seems only to be following, the kind that everyone begs to stay on. Some of Bill's gift for leadership comes from his equanimous temper, his being a prince and a mensch. And some of it—I see this as he talks about the doings of the thermosphere—comes from Bill's work in the unpredictable reaches of space, work that has prepared him to interpret, perhaps even to guide, the signals of sixty-odd citizen-gardeners engaged in the annual discussion of the Themes.

The Themes are the perennial subjects that will arise in this meeting as long as the meeting shall endure. Obviously, only initiates can know all of the Themes, as only some were prepared for the whole of the Eleusian mysteries. Decorum does not permit me to reveal the exchanges surrounding The Way Too Tall Sunflower, or the agonizing To Rototill Or Not To Rototill. But no harm can come from airing a few selected themes, say, The Bad Gardener. We never know what kind of badness it will be. That changes from year to year, as does the renegade soul. All we can know is that someone will do something completely outré. Last year it was a gardener who, it turns out, had not only a plot in our garden, but also one in a crosstown garden. Double-dipping is forbidden in a city with a long waiting list of citizens who wish to garden, so by unanimous vote, the energetic lady was banished. (And this was right, although I abstained because I was, in truth, sorry to see her go, for she had made a raised bed right next to my plot containing the tiniest, most intensely flavored strawberries.)

The subject of delinquency often leads us directly to The Untended Plot—a Theme that struggles with the question of what to do about gardeners who at some point during the season, for one of many possible reasons, let their gardens go (seemed like it would be fun; Sam said he was going to do it; transferred to Texas). The question for the assembled is, When is an abandoned plot abandoned? As you may already know, this is not the sort of question you want sixty people to consider in a consensus-style meeting on a Saturday morning, and it may be that it was questions like this one, arising among small groups of our forebears, that first gave the ancients the sweet, seemingly merciful idea of dictatorship.

Now this is a *garden*, for heaven's sake, not district court, yet there can be no sustained human activity involving sixty human beings that does not spawn its own tangled proto-politics, incipient bureaucracy, and deeply contrasting views of the Good. The divergence in this small room is vast, and mostly held in check because the majority believes that, in the long run, we will do better, will be able to grow our plants in peace, if we don't get into it too much. We make a small mistake and do get into it too much on the matter of the snaggle-toothed privet hedge—which is not really a usual Theme, but a wild card.

It starts out well. We all agree that the spaces in the hedge allow dogs and cats to slip into the garden and that this is not good. A motion is made that we buy more bushes to plug up the holes and keep out the animals. It seems like an easy call until one of our number pipes up to argue that the privet hedge is ugly ("always *has* been ugly") and that a chain-link fence would be more attractive — not only more efficient, more *attractive*. Dumbfounded looks. Murmurs. Did we hear right that there is among us a person, a tiller of the earth, who prefers chain-link to privet? Now we are launched on a free-for-all debate about fences — types of, costs of, virtues of — and Bill is making a mighty effort to bring the talk down from the thermosphere and to a vote, when a trembling but imperial voice, a voice that recalls the aged Katharine Hepburn, rings through the room:

"That hedge has been there for *years*. Years and years! Why does anyone want to take it out *now?*"

And that's that. Then Alice recalls that last year a great heap of salt marsh hay was trucked in, and asks if a load of hay is coming this year. To an outsider, this will sound like an innocent question, but everyone present knows that salt marsh hay is prelude to The Weedy Path. Ed Norberg, who often trucks in a load or two of salt marsh hay for the whole garden to use, says that he is sorry but he is not going to be hauling in salt marsh hay this year, but that we can buy it ourselves on Route 2. He tells us where. As we are taking that in, another gardener begins a quasi-manifesto about the condition of our garden paths, and how much more handsome the garden would be if the paths were weeded, and mulched with hay.

"The unweeded sections are actually dangerous!" cries an ally.

"This subject comes up every year!" chimes another gardener, galvanized. "What must we do to get compliance?"

As half the room buzzes like bees preparing to swarm, the other half begins to slink down in its folding chairs.

Someone who has great faith in the written word says, "There is a *rule* about the paths."

"Yes, but people *ignore* this rule," says a harsh realist.

Bill says, "Now, now," that serious offenders will be asked to leave the garden but that we must try a non-punitive approach. The techniques of mulching could be described in a newsletter, for instance.

But we have *tried* stressing the virtues, says the realist, who also points out that we do not *have* a newsletter.

"Now, now," says Bill.

Donna proposes that pebbles be used for the paths.

"How about asphalt?" someone murmurs.

Scott says that we could tell Ed how much salt marsh hay we want and all chip in to buy it together.

Ed reminds everyone he is not going to truck in any salt marsh hay this year.

Eric says don't get any ideas, he is not volunteering to go get the hay, but he will make a few phone calls, and does everyone want hay if he can find it?

Cathy says no, she does not want Eric's hay, because how does she know what kind of hay Eric will get, I mean does he know how to *smell* hay?

Donna says you have to make hay while the sun shines.

Jim says Eric should get the hay, but how much?

Eric says he will figure it out, and he'll either get it right or wrong, and how does Cathy smell hay?

Judy asks what *is* mulch, anyway?

Cindy says, "Okay, this is enough talk. What will we actually *do*? What we need is"—she pauses dramatically—"*a mechanism*."

"There, there," says Bill.

"It should smell good, no mold," says Cathy.

Adam stands up. "This is such a nice little community," he says. "I get nervous when we start talking about mechanisms. I'd like to rely on our human ability to just talk with the people next to us."

"But then there are all these little feuds between people," Susan counters.

A sixtyish gentleman intones, patiently (the "Now, kids" implied), "Keeping our garden paths clear and free of weeds is a *regulation*. Let's just emphasize that we all want this."

A forty-something woman, a psychologist, nods to the gentleman and says warmly, approvingly, "You're suggesting that we solve this by strengthening the social contract."

Scott proposes that it would be simple enough to put the rule about the paths in bold typeface in the newsletter.

Someone points out again that we do not *have* a newsletter.

Donna says, loudly, "I think we should all buy our vegetables at the *store*."

It works. It works well, like compost, lime, and powdered sea kelp, and when all the Themes have been addressed, the meeting adjourns and the roomful of gardeners walks outside into a cold March day. It has been snowing during the meeting, and anyone who looks down the street will see an open field with dozens of wind glistens, those small tornadoes of snow, whirling up from the field like genies out of rubbed lamps.

Two months later our gardens are green with early peas. Four months later, the days are long and hot, and in the cool of the evening, my husband and I are kneeling in our postage stamp of earth hard by an old toluene tank. We are plucking the last of the lettuce that has not already bolted into the tall, ornate pagodas of midsummer. We do buy most of our vegetables at the store, of course, but we come here for other reasons. Here we may hear an old woman with a bum heart singing Cole Porter songs among her plants. *To* them. "You're the top," she croons to some peonies, "you're the Coliseum. / You're the top, / you're the Louvre museum." Here we may talk with a family recently from Prague, who are growing sorrel for soup, whose young son is stomping along the path in a Mutant Turtle cape. The father is surprised that Peter and I don't know sorrel soup. "It is slippery," he says, "and . . . what is the word?" He looks at his wife. "Sour? No, tart. Tart. Like lemon."

Here, we stop to study an unknown; it has a slender green stem that supports a shapely Romanov dome of a bulb. Here, there is a bean that neither spins nor toils and is a Kentucky Wonder. Here, there is a spider with gold legs, spinning on one of the indeterminate vines whose heavy red globes have exploded from a seed as light as an eyelash.

STORE

‖‖ ‖‖ ‖‖

IN DECEMBER of the first year that the Bains owned Par-nel's, the mom & pop store across the street, a large wooden crate of huge, hook-necked, green-and-yellow-striped squashes sud-denly appeared in the little room. Dozens of squashes, each as big as a spade, spilled from the crate, and over the days began to colo-nize the room, migrating from the crate onto the newspaper rack, the bread shelf, the lottery ticket stand. The Haitian ladies who shop Parnel's were buying these giants by threes and fours, and I surmised that squash in some form was a winter holiday food. One morning while buying the *Globe*, I hefted one of the squashes, ad-miring its sculptural body. A woman nearby, at the canned food shelf, said, "That's *calabaza*. We call it *joumou*. It's for soup." I think she was going to tell me how to cook squash, but Joe Bain overheard from his post at the counter: "You should taste *joumou* before you cook him," he called out. "You might not like him."

The Christmas holidays came and went, and by the last day of December the large wooden squash crate was empty. New Year's Day that year was bitter cold, with the steely-gray, ruthless skies that can begin the year in coastal New England. About noon, as Peter and I sat about in the existential ruin of that first day, looking for some organizing principle that might put in a good root for the year, the doorbell rang. We opened the door and there on our front porch stood Joe Bain, holding in his arms what looked like a large fancy headdress or small ceremonial pagoda.

"This is *joumou*," Joe said, presenting a basket tied up in a linen cloth and sitting on a woven tray. "This is for the New Year, like turkey on Thanksgiving." He would not stay—he must get home, dinner is waiting—and after pressing the assemblage into our hands, Joe was off with a wave.

We bore the thing upstairs, unwrapped the cloth, lifted the basket top, and removed the ceramic lid of the bowl inside the basket. So intense was the saffron yellow color inside that the soup fairly shimmered. The soup was steaming hot, and it was midday, and so we began that year in the traditional Haitian way, eating bowls of silky purée of squash soup studded with chunks of meat, carrots, potatoes, onions, and beets. The tureen of soup lasted for a week, and by the end of that time our daily reports had convinced Alice Bain to entrust us with her recipe for *soupe de joumou*—which Joe declared to be unlike anyone else's. "Better," he said. "My wife's soup is the best," he said definitively, with the propriety of the spousal bond.

There is a notice on the front door of the store about someone who will do your income taxes, and a poster about a lost cat named Cleopatra. Once, for three months a six-foot cardboard parrot in a Hawaiian print shirt and pink sunglasses and purple sandals stood out front offering entry forms for a vacation contest—the long blue claws curling over the sandals. But the parrot faded and was taken away, and the store went back to looking like an ordinary mom & pop store on the corner. After dark, the sign on the roof gives off a cool, diffuse light—that winks in fragments through the trees of our street like lightning-bug tails: *Par...'s...en...ent... Sto...ican & Tro...ods.*

Joe Bain arrives at his store each morning at seven or seven-fifteen. He has high cheekbones and close-cropped hair. In summer he often wears khaki slacks, a tropical dress shirt, and a gold medallion around his neck. With him many mornings is a sleepy boy, who slips his fingers under the strings of two stacks of rival city papers and lugs the papers into the store. After the father unlocks the metal grill, pushes it rasping across its track, the child pulls the papers inside, touches a switch. Joe rotates a cardboard on the door from "Closed" to "Open."

A hunter-green canvas awning once shaded the store windows, but the cloth is now a faded fringe. To ward off the sun, Joe has mounted sheets of pegboard inside his two front windows. There are also several paper signs taped on the glass: "Ice Cold," reads one; "Mangoes 99¢" and "Concha y Toro."

Parnel's Convenient Store, American & Tropical Foods.

For ninety years, the store was Cormier's, after its Acadian founders. Cormiers and their cousins, the Tetraults, tended the store through a depression and two world wars and into the 1980s, when it was sold to a plump man from Delhi—Sonny, who brought chutneys and Basmati, king of rices, to our street. I liked Sonny—"Veg or non-veg?" he once asked me—but he had a feud with Peter over something neither of them could ever adequately explain, and one morning Peter found a half-dozen eggs cracked open on his pickup truck. After the egging, I spoke sternly to each of the men, feeling suddenly like a woman much older than myself, and they let the thing die down. But Sonny also ran into trouble selling beer to minors, and he gave up on the store and went home to India. For a year the store was vacant, and then one early fall day, Sonny's "For Sale" sign came down. A few weeks later, Joe and Alice Bain were stocking the shelves with Caribbean spices and drinks, with French perfumes, with tropical vegetables and fruits, and the literature of their native Haiti. The Bains also tied a little brass bell to the door.

The bell begins tinkling as soon as the store is unlocked each morning: children come in on the way to school, men and women going to work duck in for a coffee for the commute. Elderly men come for a paper and some society after their long evenings alone. One shuffles down the sidewalk in bedroom slippers, the soles of the slippers going *schhhlp schhhlp schhhlp* on the cement.

"Morning, Joe," the old man says, selecting an unwrinkled *Herald* from the rack, rarely the one on top. "How's everything?"

"Not too bad," Joe says, or "Okay," or when the weather suits him, when the air is cool and dry, he may declare, "I am grreate!" rolling the *r*'s a little.

The old man waits, fingering one of the beaded keychains in a box on the counter, and Joe says, "Everything's going to be all right."

The man nods.

"He comes every day," Joe tells me, after I chance to observe the exchange. "Not to buy. And I tell him that every day."

The owner of Parnel's Convenient Store will laugh easily but there is always a flinty alloy available to his sweet nature. He can ignore—"cut dead" an earlier generation would have called it—a city cop grousing about his van on street-cleaning day. This morning three young girls in the plaid, pleated skirts of St. John the Evangelist's school have stopped in to buy three chocolate cupcakes on their way to class. The girls are shy fifty cents, but Joe gives them all three cupcakes. "You bring it next time you come. Don't forget." As the girls leave, he says to me with a shrug, "They will forget."

A baked-goods supplier wiggles through the narrow aisle with a dolly of donuts and coffee cakes. Joe signs the bill of lading, and then in between customers offloads the boxes and stocks his baked goods shelf. By 8:30 or 9:00 A.M., Haitian women are arriving in their immaculate shopping outfits for a week's worth of rice and vegetables, and French Creole is rising from the street.

This must be a surprising turn of events for the Levesques and Bretons who still populate our neighborhood, our elderly French-Canadian neighbors whose grandparents settled these streets and built the great church on the avenue and named it Notre Dame de Pitié. Because the great American experiment continues, because a new wave of immigrants has come to this portal district, our French-speaking neighbors can once again stroll into the corner store and ask for *du lait* or *du pain* in the mother tongue. And I can practice.

"*Bonjour, Monsieur Joe, comment ça va?*"

"*Ça va. Et vous, Madame?*"

"*Ça va bien.*"

"*Il fait du vent aujourd'hui,*" I might say on a breezy day, and Joe will give me the daily lesson:

"*Il y a de la brise,*" he says. "*Pas du vent, la brise! Tu comprends?*"

When I do comprend, or make whole sentences, or introduce a new word, Joe beams solicitously.

"*Tu fais du progrès,*" my tutor says, hopefully. "*Peu à peu!*"

Joe and his wife Alice also train my accent, an accent which used to be the occasion for any of the Haitian men visiting with Joe to double over in merry peels, but recently caused the lady behind me in line to ask Joe, as I was leaving the store, "*Française?*" So I can die happy, *Dieu merci!*

The store is not a sure thing. It holds on, like the sidewalk maple so stressed by the new hydrocarbons in the air and by tall trucks crashing into its lower limbs. In the era of BJ's Discount food clubs and supermarkets, the little market on our street survives only because the Bains have designed their store to serve two tiers of customers. For proximate neighbors—we are loyal, but limited in number—Parnel's is stocked with candy bars, balls of string, batteries, milk and bacon, emergency candles, Chianti, and glitter crayons.

Who buys the speckled enamel coffee pots like the ones 1940s movie cowpokes and hoboes used at their campfires I don't know, but to draw the larger Haitian community, which is dispersed throughout the city, Joe and Alice also stock their shelves with prayer candles, Coco Rico sodas, and bottled parfums—Nuit Blanche, Rose Folie, and Champs Elysées. For these customers, dull, yellow-green stalks of sugarcane lean against the wall and island root vegetables are piled high in cardboard boxes: the brown, potato-like *yotitia* from Santo Domingo; *nagro* yams from Brazil, each one wrapped in a creamy brown paper; and pumpkin-shaped squashes from Haiti. There are boxes of plantains and green bananas, shelves of tamarind and guava nectars, packets of *senne pot*, the island culture's herb for "improving children's appetites." There is a wall of beans—*frijoles negros, habichuelas pintas, coloradas pequeñas*—and there is another wall of grains—plantain flour from Ecuador, Mais Mouline and *blé* from Haiti, rice flour, yellow corn grits, and the yellow corn flour called *acassan*. There are bins of *poisson fortement salée*, choice boned salted cod, and burlap bags of jasmine-scented rice, each bag stamped with the picture of a regal green elephant.

None of the piped-in soft pop that bludgeons the supermarket customer with relentless cheerfulness is here. It is a quiet room save for the hours during a baseball game, when the air is filled with a buzzy jangle from the television on a shelf near the baby pacifiers and rubber gloves. Often the small room is filled with conversations, some of them taking place on the phone that sits in the window, the kind of pay telephone that looks like a regular phone on steroids. By the phone is the dark green rack that holds the city's newspapers and, in this store, on the bottom shelf, a handful of copies of a small white booklet: *Pour Convertir Nos Revers En Victoires*—For Converting Our Losses into Victories—Jean Baptiste Aristide's plan to foster a government of the people, by the people, for the people in the island nation of Haiti. A how-to about what Aristide calls the *"difficile institutionnalisation démocratique."* There are passages on *"Le face-a-face avec la bourgeoisie"* and *"Des fractions diverses du duvaliérisme."*

Near the old plan there is another booklet, *Sweet Phrases for Lovers*—a handy English-Creole-French book of translations featuring a great range of the utterances necessary for a romance, from "May I kiss your hand?" (*Mwen met embrose men ou ?/ Puis-je baiser la main?*) to "First of all, you do not even have a donkey, you are lazy, you do not want to work and you think you're in love with a young lady!" (*Pou koumanse, ou pa menm genyen tou tibourik ale we pouoto! Jan ou parese, ou pa menm vle travay epi w bezwen renmen farnm!*).

Near the literature of liberation and love there is always a box of fresh loaves of Le Foyer dough bread, and under a plastic dome, a stack of sticky, golden-brown coconut cakes. Really big temptations are kept behind the counter: lottery tickets are doled out of a wooden drawer to adults who come in with two or forty dollars and buy a single cardboard or long sheaves of gold-and-red foil tickets named Red Hot, High Roller, Mystery Money. Candy is meted out from a behind the counter to small children, actual tykes, who come in with a quarter and begin to learn just how much of the sweet world their coin equals. Lately they want spun sugar shaped in green and white rings, and gelatinous squiggles called worms.

Mid-afternoon, when I cross the street again for a Coke (that brown wine of America), a meek drunk is putting a quart of beer down on the glass-top counter. He's on his way home from work, bits of red hair stick out from his paint cap, maroon paint on his coveralls. Joe slips the bottle into a brown bag, twists the soft Kraft paper around the neck, takes the man's dollars. "You could stop," he says, handing over the package. Softly, matter of factly, like he's saying "The Bears are playing tonight." The man hears the tone, doesn't get angry. "I know it," he says. Joe treads one more step, "There's a program at the hospital." "I'm going to do it someday," says the wavering man. "You'll see, you'll be amazed at me," and weaves out of the store, upends the packet in the sun. "He can't drink at all," Joe says. "He's a good man, but he just can't drink at all." Joe shrugged his shoulders the day he said, "I am going to have to do it," meaning he couldn't make the store profitable without the income from beer and wine. "Don't come back," he growls at underage kids who try to buy from his store, "and don't go somewhere else."

Alice Bain, who works at a hospital, keeps the Convenient Store on Sundays and sells the tower of Sunday papers. "Zhoe is terrible," Alice declared one afternoon in amused mock anger, upon learning that Joe had not passed on to her some tidbit of information from me. "Zhoe tell me nothing from the customer!" (Though he must have told her about one customer's interest in a squash.) But it is true that Joe's sense of formality makes him reluctant to carry social messages back and forth, and it is Alice who speaks of the daughter's drum and bugle corps competitions, the son who was asked to be an altar boy at Speaker O'Neill's funeral, the older boys in college, how one has lost a little weight.

The idea of store that the Bains brought to our street is the closest thing this neighborhood has to a public living room. Here the disappearance of Cleopatra is announced. Here neighbors sign the petition to keep a chain donut place from opening near Verna's Coffee Shop. Here events in Haiti are debated. Here flyers are posted for meetings about the toxins in our soil and water table. Here customers and the Bains offer each other pleasantries, opinions about Dennis Rodman's hair; cloned sheep; the Mars landing; the growing gap between rich and poor; the folly, not to mention the inhumanity of no guaranteed health insurance; the growing gap; odds of winning the lottery; how terrific Halloween was this year (balmy, and oh, that Carmen Miranda with a fruit basket on her head, that little tiger). Over the years, Alice and Joe have seen the neighborhood soul as well as anyone save perhaps the local priests.

The Bains would be uncommon in any era, but their kind of store was once a commonplace. Parnel's Convenient is the last survival of dozens of small markets that dotted our neighborhood from about 1870 until the 1950s. Alice Harrington, who has lived two houses from the Convenient Store for seventy-one of her seventy-four years, remembers all of the former markets. I first met Alice Harrington one day in May when we were both out sweeping. Annually, Alice sweeps enough of the neighborhood walk to be on the payroll of the department of public works. "Hullo," she called that day, waving with her broom. I walked across the street and down three houses to her station. "I don't know why people think street cleaning is all up to the city," Alice huffed. I said I didn't either, and felt myself being admitted to the society of the broom. We stood with our long wood-and-straw wands (Alice was using a Big Chief) and later that month she invited me over for tea.

"There was always a store on the corner where Joe is now," she says. "There was another store where the social club is now. It was tiny too, but it was called the First National, and the man in charge was Pat Haley . The next store was a meat market, and that man's name was Cohen. Next was a shoemaker, then the barber, and next there was Milio, who had all this nice Italian pasta. He would have it in different bins and measure it out for you. Oh, that was good."

Alice recalls how she used to play in the street, hopscotch, jump rope, and hide and seek. "But that stopped," she says, "after the war, when the cars came." "When the cars came" is one woman's perfect, succinct history of the massive change from a city criss-crossed by horsecars and streetcars to the automobile city. With a car, supermarkets made sense, and the Milios and Pat Haleys closed up shop. "We can't have it all," Alex Marshall said recently in the *Washington Post* (though I think it's been said before). "The clerk at the Circuit City who sells you a washing machine . . . will not know your name. It is a tradeoff. For the most efficient distribution system in the modern world, for the elimination of all middlemen, we get a life almost devoid of intimate contact between the home and the market."

One afternoon I chanced to ask Joe where the food in his store comes from, meaning the place where Joe actually picks up his inventory. The more complex question, answerable only by tracing through granaries, warehouses, and freighters, and faraway fields, I was not asking, which Joe realized, for he said, "Chelsea"— which is two towns over, by the Mystic River, the site of the New England central produce market. He's surprised I want to go, but agrees to take me. A few days later at 4:30 A.M. his van pulls up in front of my porch and we drive several miles to the produce market. We will spend two hours in the vast complex, as Joe bargains, selects papayas, lettuces, tomatoes, avocados, potatoes, stacks boxes in his van—both of us threading steadily through schools of miniature forklifts, machines called palette jacks (or just jacks) that scoot through the market like swift squids, emitting a high, soft electronic call. It is a world of produce stevedores and big-rig drivers working deals with wholesalers, everyone dealing at a dead run, everyone wearing baseball caps, the stevedores in leather weight-lifting belts with a flag, or heart, or lightning bolt burned into the leather. Summing up the scene, one of the produce men says, "Okay, you've got the Mushroom People, the Tomato People, the Potato People, the Celery Hearts People, and the Onion People."

I have to run to keep up with Joe as he ducks into the bays of companies named Boston Banana, Marco Tomato, Arthur Silk; the Brothers Forlizzi, Matarazzo, and Dolci; Arrow Farms, Gold Bell, and Pro-Deuce. Each of the bays is huge and refrigerated, and the scent in the air will be a mingling of wet cardboard and pineapple, or cardboard and corn, or oranges, or mangoes, or the hard, heavy yams that come packed in a mass of their own damp, rust-colored roots. Posters on the walls of the bays picture not women in seductive poses, not sports heroes, not fast cars, but ravishing tropical fields, clusters of kiwis, perfect bananas.

The foods are the color of flame. They are nut-brown, tawny, ruddled, pea- and grass-green. They are damson and plum, and none is a single color, but is flecked, veined, or brindled. They are turning color before your eyes, perishable with life. It must be different than selling duct tape or flanges, though in market jargon the botanical kaleidoscope undergoes a metamorphosis. One of the Apple People, recalling a recent visit from a foreign trade delegation, says to us, "The Russian minister was going from bay to bay. And boy oh boy, he ate so much product!" A Celery Person tells me, "Most of our business is hearts, but we also sell product to Chinese restaurants." A Tomato Man says, "The main question is, How much product can we move?" Note that "product," the transmodal integer, takes no article, no "the," or "a," or "an." "Product" is pure placeholder.

Leaving the last store, Joe wheels a laden trolley down a steep incline, bracing its weight with his body. He has been embarrassed by my offers to help him lift a few boxes from dock to van, and each time I hand him a box he says, "No, no, I can do this. No, no, that one he is too heavy." This is the sixth round of boxes he has loaded into the van, whose volume is now filled. The morning shop is complete. On the two days each week that my neighbor goes to the produce market (and the third day a week that he goes to the meat market), this is his regime: Awake at four A.M.; at the market by five-fifteen; shop until about seven; head home to pick up the youngest children and get them to school by seven-thirty. Minutes later, Joe is pulling up in front of his store. He will spend several hours unloading his van in between tending to customers, and will keep the store until nine P.M., when we hear the steel grate rasp over the door. (Seventeen, if you are counting.)

"It's hard work, Joe," I say as we cross the river heading back toward our neighborhood. "It is hardest in the winter," he says, not disagreeing. "Some days the roads are not plowed, and I never get used to the cold. But the produce workers are always there, every morning when it opens, no matter if it is snowing or ice. Always there," Joe says, describing his own work ethic too. Passing the marshes along the Mystic River, Joe says, "If it is for the profit, I can close the store tomorrow. But all the time, when people come to the store . . . well, this is what I will say: joy is a thing that you can create in your life. Because when you find some place you enjoy, and you find great people, that is a riches."

We had known each other for five years before Joe could talk about Haiti. The few times that I broached the subject Joe grew uneasy, casting his eyes around protectively as we stood in the complete privacy of his own store. I stopped asking, and wondered whether it was the long reach of a military junta, or something closer to home, here within our borders, that could cause a rock-steady man to go jittery. And then one morning Joe's surprising reply to *"Bonjour, Monsieur, ça va?"* is "My father owned a big bakery in Haiti. When I was nineteen years old, he send me to Paris to study business, and when he get to be an old man he want me to take over and run the bakery. But I was young and I want to do something different."

"Racontes-moi," I say and fold the *Globe* in my arms and lean against the wall and soon we have left the store with its wall display of dried herbs and baby pacifiers, and we are in a countryside where a young Joe Bain is buying *vetyver* from farmers.

I had always assumed that vetiver itself was something—flower, animal hoof, vegetable oil?—that emanated from Provence, or was perhaps distilled directly from the Parisian air. I got this idea because a company named Roget & Gallet wraps its *vetyver*-scented savons parfumés in pleated tissue, then seals each bar with gold foil and nests three of these jewels inside a box that looks as much like a Louis Seize inlaid table as a cardboard box can look. Now I learn from Joe that vetiver does not come from Paris, nor even from France, but from Haiti, from the root of the Khuskus grass, Vetiveria zizaniodes. "A big green bushy grass," says Joe, "with a good root. The root hold the oil."

Joe named his company Spéculateur, and set up several depots in the provinces—stations where farmers could come to sell their stacks of the precious root. With a team of men and fleet of trucks, Joe transported the root stocks to a manufactory in Port au Prince. There the oil was extracted and then shipped to the great parfumeries of Paris and New York. Joe describes the technique of gathering the root: "The farmer must cut it when it is just ready," he says. "They must not pick him up too young. What does it look like? The root look just like the hair of grass in the ground. It go deep deep in the ground, and he spread. After the farmers get the root out of the ground, they shake him off and put him in the sun. When he is dry, they tie him up, and make a big bunch, and then they bring him to me. This is a very good business," Joe says. "All the parfumeries get their vetyver oil from Haiti. Right now, I have a friend in Port au Prince who makes the oil and sends it to France. He has about five hundred people working for him. He started the same year as me, the same time. You know," Joe says evenly, "I didn't want to come to the United States when I was in the vetyver business. If I didn't have those people harassing me . . ." He shakes away the thought.

Roaming his first homeland, Joe has been smiling, gone on one of memory's weightless journeys. Along the way, he remembers something else, and when he is finished talking about vetiver, he says with no transition, "People think there was no democracy in

Haiti, but before Duvalier, there *was* democracy." In Joe's accent, the word is "day-mo-*cra*-see" — a pronunciation that makes the old ideal sound new and fresh, the kind of refreshment democracy does, in fact, always need.

"I was born one year after the occupation." He's referring to the U.S. occupation of Haiti from 1915 to 1935. "In my time," Joe says, "Haiti was one hundred percent democracy. Democracy is respect each other; that's what it is about. *We had that.* When there were disagreements, people go to the courts, and they will find justice in them. I serve on the jury in two murder cases. In one case, a young man murder an old woman. She was living alone and he think that maybe she have money. I was elected the president of the jury and I think that if I give the death penalty, I am a murderer too. I am no better. So, we give the man a life-in-jail sentence. And the same with the other case."

My neighbor would be in Haiti still, a prominent *homme d'affaires* and dispenser of justice, the kind of man the Haitians call *un notable,* had not a handful of the Tonton Macoutes, the thugs of Papa Doc Duvalier's U.S.-backed regime, paid a call. They came one day to invite Joe to join the government. Papa Doc, they said, could use an enterprising man, a natural leader. Joe declined and Duvalier's men came again to issue the invitation. Again Joe refused. And then the men came at night. "I was wearing no shoes, and only shorts, and they took me away to the police station. I keep asking, 'What have I done? I don't know anything I have done.'" What Joe had done, of course, was support someone other than Duvalier. In 1957, when Joe was twenty, he worked for Louis deJoe's election. "He is the one the people want to be President," Joe remembers. "But the army stole the election from deJoe, and give it to Duvalier. Now Duvalier was not popular, but he has the support of the bourgeoisie and the military. And," Joe continues in an understatement worthy of an ambassador, "I believe there was an order from the United States for Duvalier, and that is how the army stole the election from deJoe."

When the Tonton Macoutes let him go, Joe Bain sold his trucks, his house, and his stocks of vetiver. He married Alice on Friday, came to America on Saturday. Many lives were lost in those years, but it was not fear, Joe says, that prompted him to leave. "It was a humiliation. It was a humiliation for a government to do that to a citizen who was working hard for a living. I haven't done anything wrong, in fact I was *helping* the government because I have about twenty guys working for me. I'm helping the government! But it was not government," he says. "It was dictatorship. Even in a dictatorship, they cannot make *all* the people obey. Not everyone can see, but I see what it was in Haiti then—and I like to stand."

First he lived in Manhattan, then Alice came too, and the Bains moved to Boston. Joe's story continues as he remembers exactly how much—$1.85, $2.10, $3.50—he earned per hour in a series of jobs during his first years in America. He recites the rates, the overtime work, the gradual advancement, how it helped that he had been to business school in Paris. It is a blur to my ears even in the moment, but each fifty cents from two decades ago is fresh and inscribed in Joe's inner calculation. Perhaps I would be getting more of it if I weren't still stopped in my tracks by that earlier phrase, that simple phrase said in the cadenced voice: "I like to stand."

The paper I had been holding that morning was full of news from Haiti—one story about the military elite, who did not then believe that the U.S. would move to usurp their power, and another about the many Haitian-Americans who believe that the last thing the U.S. wants in their native land is a real democracy. "Why do some people in the United States want to ruin Haiti?" Joe asks the air one day, puzzled by the sheer illogic of it. Joe is a viscerally political man of a political people who enjoy the tradition of debate and individual opinion. He distinguishes expertly between the diverse strains of American policy and how they variously affect his first homeland. Recent Republican administrations he sums up with one word: "*Diables!* They were sending arms every day to the army. They *kill* the people! But most of the time," he reflects, "you should hold it in your chest. The truth will never be able to spell out. And a lot of people don't like to hear the truth. Maybe ten years from now we can see democracy again in Haiti. It is still very hard, but a few years ago people were being tortured. Compared with that, right now is a paradise in Haiti. It is slow, but many people are working on it seriously, and God is not sleeping."

Suddenly Joe adds, "Do you want to know what makes *joumou* our tradition for New Year's Day?"

"*Mais oui!*"

"When the Haitian people were slaves, only the French were allowed to eat squash and cow. So when Haiti become independent—this is on January first, 1804—they kill a cow. All over the country, the former slaves make a feast of cow and squash. That is the reason we have the tradition of squash soup with beef in the New Year. You know that Haiti helped the United States fight for independence? Yes! We send men to fight with the American colonists for independence, and only twenty-nine years later, we have our own independence. You see how we have been *participating* in the fight for independence for a long time."

At nine P.M., when the streets are dark, Joe cuts off the lights inside the Convenient Store, pulls the metal grill over the door and padlocks the grate. At this hour in summer the red and lime-green Concha y Toro sign filters through the leaves of our maple, and here and there a partial phrase—"merican & Tropi"— glows like one of the bioluminescent fishes in inky water. And then we all sleep. And then comes the rasp of the grille being pulled aside in a fine rain, and Joe is unwrapping newspapers from their plastic jackets, shaking the plastic, sending a miniature shower of water beads onto his linoleum floor. Frank Dewey comes in lowering a black umbrella, and Joe, bending over the fresh news, hands the old man a dry *Herald* from the middle of the heap.

ALICE BAIN'S
SOUPE DE JOUMOU

Ingredients
2 lbs. beef stew meat
1 large *joumou* (if not available, a hubbard or acorn squash
    will do)
4 onions
4 stalks celery
3 carrots
1 green pepper
parsley
watercress, cabbage, or beets (or any vegetable desired)
4–6 cups of stock
tomato paste
any spices, especially garlic (3–5 large cloves)

Cut a large *joumou* squash in half, take out the seeds, and bake
the squash for about an hour or until the inside is tender. When
it has cooled, scrape out the squash and purée it. Meanwhile,
prepare the beef as if you were making stew: cut the beef into
small chunks and brown them with green peppers, celery, and
onions. When the meat is brown, add some tomato paste. Com-
bine the squash purée and the meat and vegetable mixture with
several cups of stock. Bring to a boil, then simmer for forty-five
minutes, adding the parsley, carrots, any other vegetables, garlic
(minced or pressed) to the soup, along with salt and pepper, and
curry flavoring as desired.

Serve on New Year's Day.

S I G N

━━━━━━━

〜〜 〜〜 〜〜

JUST BEFORE our triple-decker became home, an inspector came to look it over. He found a nest of carpenter ants that
"should be checked out right away," but said systems were fine, that
the tar and gravel roof would last several more years. The one thing
that troubled the home inspector, that made him stare and take me
aside, was the missing foundation. It wasn't *all* missing, as the
young real estate agent pointed out, and he seemed on the verge of
calling it a rustic foundation, a foundation with potential. But the
inspector, an older man who wore a flannel shirt and a corduroy
jacket, peered sharply over his glasses at the younger man, who
grudgingly agreed that the house did not have all the foundation
you would want, ideally, in a new home.

I was glad for the inspector's concern, of course, but had assumed that the gaping hole in the base of the prospective house
would be repaired before dollars and title were exchanged,
whereas the home inspector did not. And that must be one of the
many reasons that we have home inspectors. In fact, the sellers
were perfectly decent and did plan to repair the hole, but they had
been slowed in some insurance company labyrinth as the company tried, as I did now, to figure out what, exactly, had happened.

It seemed that this house on the corner of two sleepy one-way streets, a candidate for home, had been rammed by a fuel oil truck. There were extenuating circumstances—a shaggy privet hedge, a row of illegally parked cars—but the main point is that the driver had cheated, had not stopped at his stop sign before sailing into the intersection. Instantly, the truck driver must have seen that his behemoth was about to crush a VW bug which was also advancing through the crossing—in the case of the bug, legally. An eyewitness said that the truck driver had swerved mightily and had avoided the small car by a hair before he lost control of the truck, crashed through a hedge, and rammed the nearest house.

Shortly after the inspector's visit, a mason appeared with a diamond-shaped trowel and a vat of a thick gray magma. When his work was done the home inspector returned and saw that it was good. "Look at this," he said, running his hand over the cement, admiring the seam and color. "It's a perfect match. You're all set now, lady," he said. "Best of everything to you." He didn't call "Hi-yo, Silver, away!" but it was like that, and I was grateful to him and to the mason, whose works were like a civil benediction on the house.

Several months later, when I was installed on the third-floor flat of that house, a caterwaul of squeals erupted in the street, followed by a grim thud. Below, two cars sat in the crossing—one of them steaming, both crumpled like sheets of tinfoil. Drivers staggered out. Police arrived. Calls were made, and one mother and one taxicab came. The drivers were only shaken, although their cars were now abstract sculptures. What a fluke, I thought, and then thought no more of it until one morning a few months later there was a blare of horns and a shivery crash. And then again, two months after that, and then again . . . There were bad bruises, cuts, sprains, screams, lost time, anger, confusion, and guilt, but, remarkably, no one was ever badly injured.

Sometimes after the accident, a dazed man or woman, a teenager or child came and sat on my front porch to wait for a tow truck, an aunt, the police, a boyfriend. I offered what I could—washcloths, a telephone, tissues. Once I drove a frightened, sobbing girl home. "My father is going to kill me," she said. That didn't sound good and we talked and it turned out that her father probably wouldn't kill her, but for sure she would be grounded and miss Lanie's party. "God, I'll die if I miss Lanie's party."

By the time five or six accidents had occurred in the intersection, I had seen how it always happened: how the unpruned hedge, the row of parked cars, the poor visibility, the deceptive sleepiness of the streets, could all conspire to lure a lax driver to ignore the stop sign. And I had thought about the word "stop," a short word though not always a simple one, as every addict, televangelist, thief, and anyone who has listened to a small child recounting a movie plot knows.

After a while I even realized who in the city was most aware of the danger posed by this innocent-looking Bermuda triangle of an intersection. So the day after an ambulance finally had to come, I sat down and wrote out a letter to one of the city councilors, the one who then lived down the street. The key phrases of the communication were "always pleased to vote for you," "condition partly to blame," "enough warning," "certain death," and "always pleased to vote for you."

In every life, let there be at least one response so satisfying as that prompted by this brief letter. The lumbering *pas de deux* of citizen and bureaucracy commenced. There was a meeting with the Councilor and the Traffic Commissioner himself, an imposing,

Babar-like man, who, it became clear during the course of the meeting, has the whole of the city mapped in his large head. Soon afterwards, three of his staff came and stood on our corner with clipboards, watching traffic and drinking coffee from a thermos. In due course, a crew from the Department of Public Works arrived on our street to install not only an additional stop sign at the intersection, but a sign a block *before* the crossing—a sign to announce a sign.

For many years now since the new signs went up, at least one member of any pair of drivers approaching the intersection at the same moment has stopped. This fleck of infrastructure, this anonymous piece of heavy-gauge sheet metal, has worked like a charm. It may almost be safe to say that whoever was going to die in the intersection is alive—is buying a bag of nails at a hardware store, using the word "galvanized"; is playing Tito Puente; is listening to a friend speak about the calming presence of our mothers, to another call the eggplant "a buxom vegetable." The alive person may be admiring a shoe made of open wire, the lightest foot, the one that Calvino has asked us to have as we step into the millennium. The alive person may be in a museum, passing an old painting of the senior and junior arbiters of fate and their assistants, the overly eager dragons. She may pause in front of a ninth-century Chinese picture of the planet deity Mercury, who is a woman attended by a monkey with a blushing red face and soft fur. (As he holds up an inkwell for the planet that governs documents, how hard that monkey tries to be good—but we all know that his tail will dip in the ink anyway.)

It's a single, simple stop sign. It is nothing compared to the infrastructure that Nan Dean Blackman caused to happen over the acres of Tuscaloosa County. Still, I like to look on the red directness of the sign, its simplicity and power pulsing day and night in all weathers, the word itself nearly two feet tall. Of all the words that I have helped to write, it is the largest and—sobering realization this—the one that serves the world most faithfully, unambiguously. And yet, being anthologized by the street is surely not a bad thing—for while life is short, the Department of Public Works is long.

NEON EFFECTS

〰〰〰〰〰〰〰〰〰〰〰〰〰〰

At times all I need is a brief glimpse, an opening in the midst
of an incongruous landscape, a glint of lights in the fog, the
dialogue of two passersby . . . and I think that, setting out
from there, I will put together, piece by piece, the perfect
city, made of fragments . . . of signals . . .

— Italo Calvino, *Invisible Cities*

"Do you want to know what I think?" Tommy asks, mildly
and not rhetorically but offering his customer the small window of
free will, the chance to *not know* what already burdens Tommy's su-
perior automotive mind.

What Tommy Hoo thinks has rarely been apparent in the eight
years that he and Steve Yuen and their pals at Nai Nan Ko Auto Service have cared for my Subaru three-door coupe. No, normally one
must urge Tommy and Steve to say what they think, posing brutally
direct questions: "Do I need a new battery before winter or not?" "Is
the gurgle in the transmission trouble or not?" Even when Tommy
and Steve do answer, they convey a sense that the jury is still out on
the beloved Western idea "cause and effect." They have a bone-
deep respect for the contingency of all things, and have never before actually volunteered a definitive opinion. This is an unprece-
dented moment in our relationship.

"Do you want to know what I think?"

"Yes, yes," I murmur.

Encouraged, my mechanic declares, firmly and unambiguously, "Don't put it on your car."

What I want to put on my car came as a gift from Peter, who was with me the palmy summer night that I saw a medium-size UFO floating down Brighton Avenue, hovering on a cushion of clear blue light that came billowing from underneath the craft—an airy, etherealizing light, shedding a serene glow over the asphalt road and its scurrying film of detritus. Some of us have been half-hoping for this all our lives, those of us who as children crept out after bedtime on summer nights, who stood in our backyards barefoot in the mowed grass to look up at the implacable dark glittering. And we have been well prepared for the moment in the close of darkened movie theatres; the special effects teams of Spielberg and Lucas have taught us, shown us, how to experience an encounter. We grow quiet, we suspend yet more disbelief, we feel a naive awe and a shiver of fear as the Mother Ship appears, huge and resplendent with lights beyond our ken, and again when the fragile, more-advanced-than-us beings step out into our atmosphere. But we think it will happen far away—if it happens at all—in a remote desert, on some lonely country road, to someone else. We are not prepared for this astonishment to visit our own city street, to publicly glide past the Quickie Suds and Redbone's Bar-B-Que. Now Peter has pulled up close to the hovercraft and I can see inside its glowing body. There, not abducted, are two teenage boys such as our own planet produces.

"It's a Camaro," Peter says.

It is. A late model silver Camaro to which the boys have Done Something—something that washed over me, as Philip Larkin said of jazz, the way love should, "like an enormous yes."

And now Tommy has said, "Don't put it on your car," pronouncing where Tommy has never before pronounced.

"It" is two neon tubes which mount on the underside of a car and create a ravishing fusion of color and light whenever you flick a switch on the dashboard. The effect—"The Ultimate Effect" it says on the package—is produced by an underbody lighting kit which consists of the neon tubes, mounting hardware, and a fat wad of wiring. This kit is one of the thousands of devices collectively known as "automotive aftermarket products": sound systems, sunroofs, drink-holders, mudflaps, seat covers, carpeting, coats for nose grills, and ice machines. (And, I like to think, bud vases.) One nice thing about the genre of aftermarket products is that it opens up what might have otherwise seemed closed and finite. Implicit in every aftermarket product is the idea that a vehicle is never a *fait accompli*; rather, its manufacturer has merely stopped fabrication at a reasonable point and has delivered a work-in-progress—a canvas.

The present canvas has the contour of a lithe sedan, but within that contour lies a hatchback that gives the sleek sedan the carrying capacity of a pickup truck. The rear window is a marvel of the glassmaker's art, an immense, gently curving expanse that arcs snugly over the chassis like the canopy of an F-16 over its Blue Angel. I have come with this car and the kit to Tommy and Steve because I trust them, and because their shop is so nearby that I can walk over whenever Tommy calls to say "You *cah* is ready," in his crisp, then soft, muscular speech which accents unexpected syllables, often with a faint gust of air—the sounds and emphases of Chinese overlaying English and giving it a gently pneumatic texture.

It helps to be able to *walk* to the garage of an auto mechanic whose wall is covered with letters of praise and satisfaction. It is one of the village-scale civilities that can be found in the urban world, a place that can be an impersonal tale, not least because of the automobile itself, the ways it reconfigures lives, flattens the depth of space, blurs time. So I don't want to go to another mechanic across town. I want to work with Tommy and Steve on this. When we talked over the telephone, Tommy had said, "No, we don't do that." And then he paused and asked, "Is it a *pinstripe?*" and, as always, his tone conveyed that we were only beginning, together, to enter into another automotive mystery.

Seeing the opening, I replied, "Oh no, it's not a pinstripe, it's just a couple of neon tubes mounted on the undercarriage. I could almost do it myself." (An outrageous lie if taken literally, but Tommy took my meaning: that the operation would be child's play for his shop.) "But there *is* some wiring to hook up, and I wouldn't want to mess with the electrical system."

"No, we don't do that."

I didn't say anything, and then Tommy said, "Why don't you bring over. We will take look."

One look at the kit, however, and Tommy and Steve are dead against it, and the reason is rust. "Rust," they intone together, as clerics of old must have said "Grim Reaper"—capitals implied in bitter homage. Here is the problem: to install the Ultimate Effect, a row of holes must be drilled on the undercarriage of the car, and this, my clerics believe, is an open invitation to the corroding enemy. Moreover, on this car the rocker panels offer the only site on which to mount the tubes, which fact gives us reason to say "rocker panels" several times (and me to remember a charged scene in *The French Connection*), but it must not be a good thing because the faces of Tommy and Steve remain glum.

The men also point out that the kit instructions say: "IF YOUR AREA EXPERIENCES SNOW AND ICY CONDITIONS, YOU MUST REMOVE THE SYSTEM BEFORE THE WINTER SEASON." Needless to say, New England experiences these conditions, yet it would seem simple enough to remove neon tubes each November and remount them in April (dark when Persephone descends, illuminated when she rises). But Tommy notes that no quick-release clamp system is provided with the kit, and points out that he is not inclined to jury-rig one.

"Half-hour to take off, half-hour to install. Each time," he says funereally.

The two mechanics and I stand and look at one another politely, the current automotive mystery now fully declared. After another moment Tommy says softly, kindly, "Miss *Hie*stan', this will not add to the *val*ue of *you cah*."

After a long moment peering at each other as across a gulf, I venture an explanation.

"It's for fun," I say.

"For fun," Nai Nan Ko's mechanics repeat slowly, skeptically. And then, nimbly, before my very eyes, they begin to absorb the new concept.

"For fun," they say to each other. And now they are smiling and trying very hard not to smile, nearly blushing and bashful, and unable to look at me directly. We have unexpectedly stepped over into some new and intimate territory.

Upon reflection, one knows why these men did not consider fun at the first. Commonly I appear, as all their customers do, in a stoic, braced attitude awaiting the estimate, or later in miserly ponderings: Can the brake repair be put off a few weeks? (No.)

Would a less expensive battery be okay? (No.) Fun has not come up during our eight years of dealings, not once. And now optional tubes that cost a bundle to install, tubes that tempt fate, that add no value, do not strike Tommy and Steve as barrels of it.

In the new silence that steals over us as we stand about the neon kit, I mention that it is a gift from my husband, that I will have to talk with him about the rust problem. At this piece of information, the situation transforms. Immediately, Tommy and Steve are smiling at me directly and sympathetically, relieved to be able to believe that I am on a wifely errand of humoring. In a near jolly mood, Steve stows the kit in the trunk of my car, and when last I see the two mechanics they are huddled, brooding happily under the raised hood of a bunged-up Civic.

I am also left to brood. Here is dull old duality, posing its barbaric polarity: radiant swoon or structural integrity. Shrinking from the horrible choice, it occurs to me that someone must know how to do this, that the fine mechanics of Nai Nan Ko may simply not know the tricks that New England's custom shops have devised to deal with neon and rust, neon and winter, even as MIT's particle physicists do not necessarily know how to keep a cotton-candy machine from jamming. Sure enough, Herb, at the Auto Mall in Revere, knew all about neon effects.

"Four tubes or two? For two tubes, lady, that will be three hours, a hundred and fifty to install." And he is emphatic about rust, roaring out "No problem!" One of America's mantras and a phrase that wants a whole essay for itself. *

---

*Glancingly, one can say of "No problem!" that its subtext is often a radical laissez-faire-ism, the speaker's Mr. Magoo-esque state of mind, which triggers a semantic backfire, making you think, This guy may not only *not* solve any existing problem, he may cause an en-

"None at all?" I persist. "Won't the holes allow water to seep in, especially during the winter when the tubes are out?"

"Well, sure," Herb replies peevishly, "a little water is going to get in, but it's not going to rot out right away, maybe in the *future* or sometime. Hold on a minute, lady. Eddie!" Herb calls into his shop. "That guy with the black Saturn gets his CD-changer installed in the trunk." Then back to me. "Where were we?"

"About the underbody rusting," I prompt, but greatly savoring the sound of Herb's Future—a place where rust *does* occur but whose temporal locus is so indeterminate as to make precautions about it absurd.

"See," says Herb, "I use a non-acid silicon sealant and we prime the holes with a primer."

Pressing the harried Herb one more degree, I ask if he has devised a quick-release system for the tubes for winter removal.

"Naaah," Herb replies. "I've never taken one off. They just leave 'em on."

"Really?" I ask. "But these instructions say that ice and snow destroys the neon tubes."

"Yeah, maybe," says Herb. "But I've never taken them off for anybody. *Nobody* takes them off in the winter." As an afterthought, he adds, "And that's when they get wrecked."

And that's when they get wrecked. In a tone that means, winter is the time, lady, when neon tubes on cars are *supposed* to get wrecked, Ecclesiastically speaking.

"Anything else?" Herb asks.

---

tirely new one. The term is also used now in situations where previously a speaker would have been expected to say "You're welcome." And this second usage creates a curious sensation, introducing into the exchange of simple courtesies the idea of some problem, albeit one that is, for the moment, absent.

A hard frost comes to the old Puritan city, and then winter, and the *tubos de neon* lie in their box along with the manual in Spanish and English, the high-voltage transformer, the rocker switch, fifty feet of black cable, six nylon clamps, six black *tuberia termocontraible*, eight hex screws, and *la cable de energia rojo*. There is a time for everything: a time for seeking a neon mechanic, and a time to just read the manual instead and wait for spring, even as gardeners all over our region are curling up under quilts with the Book of Burpee. The first instruction, printed in large capital letters at the top of page one, is "*SOLO PARA EL USO FUERA DE LA CARRETERA O EN EXHIBICIONES* / FOR OFF-ROAD OR SHOW USE ONLY."

Taken seriously, it would void the whole project.

The scroll of warnings continues. "*El transformador para el Sistema de Luz de Neón produce un voltaje muy alto. Proceda con cautela durante la instalacion para evitar una descarga electrica o heridas.*" Meaning, you can die of electrical shock doing this, so seriously listen up: Do not mount the effect at all on vehicles with antilock braking systems. Do not install the wiring too close to the gas tank, in consideration of the five-to-nine-thousand *voltaje muy alto*. Always always turn off the effect at gas stations when refueling. In the same large, all-caps typeface used for its death-warnings, the manual stresses one crucial aesthetic pointer. "KEEP THE NEON UNITS ABOVE THE LOWEST POINTS OF THE CHASSIS TO HIDE THEM," the manual instructs. "YOU WANT JUST THE GLOW TO BE SEEN, NOT THE UNITS THEMSELVES." This is first-rate advice that the Luminists and the Hudson River Valley School would recognize at once—all those painters who knew to locate the source of their bathing light just *beyond* the dark sail, the looming crag, the fringe of native firs.

I look up from page three (how to use a cigarette lighter to melt the *tuberia termocontraible* to make a watertight seal), and the only thing aglow outside is a streetlight in the dull gray cowl of a cold January. And yet there is a somewhere where the neon season never ends: South Florida, whose tropical climate and car culture, whose fancy for sheen and the night were destined to have brought neon and cars together at some point in the twentieth century.

The provenance of neon on wheels is traceable to Hialeah and the dragsters who first began to substitute neon tubing for the wiring on their distributors—Whoa! That lights up the whole engine block! Maybe Steve Carpenter saw that, the photographer who rigged up some temporary tubes under a Ferrari Testarossa and took a picture of the result for the album cover of a "Miami Vice" soundtrack. The general idea had gotten into the air, and the air was being inhaled, and all awaited the brothers Efrain and Roberto Rodriguez.

During one of the boreal storms that shudder into our region, I place a long-distance call to their shop in Miami. Deirdre Rodriguez answers the telephone and over the next twenty minutes tells me that her husband, Efrain, is out in the warehouse right now overseeing a shipment to Tokyo; that the fire-loving countries of Latin America, China, and Japan are her best new customers; that, of *course* she has neon on her car! ("What do you think, darling?!"); that she has a special pink-to-purple-to-magenta spectrum, and that her mother has one too! Mrs. Rodriguez, who speaks in the clipped accent of her native England, remembers the hour of advent.

"I will tell you a woman-to-woman comment," she says, lowering her voice. "This is how it really happened. One night, we were lying in bed reading, and my husband said, 'Deirdre dear, I am going to put neon under cars.' Well, neon is so very fragile, isn't it? Sometimes our installers cannot even transport the tubes to the job sites without breaking them. So I said to him, 'Darling, go back to sleep.' Poor thing, I thought, he has completely snapped."

But within a week, says Mrs. Rodriguez (nibbling a little crow), the brothers had one tube of purple neon installed under Roberto's car. "Incredible!" Mrs. Rodriguez recalls of the sight. "We were speechless." On the spot, she says, her husband and his brother understood that "they must do something." Over the next months, Efrain and Roberto spent hours experimenting in their sign shop, where they invented a way to encase neon tubes in heavy-gauge plastic cylinders, figured how to bundle the tubes with a compact transformer and how to lay out the wiring system under a chassis. By spring they were ready, and at the Miami Grand Prix the Rodriguez brothers presented the Glow Kit.

Miami saw and Miami approved in a citywide supernova of enthusiasm, which was to be expected. In less warm blooded places, neon has been a symbol for a garish modernity: "The neon glow from those technological New Jerusalems beyond the horizons of the next revolution," sniffs Aldous Huxley. But Miami knows better. She seems always to have known, intuitively, that this emanation from a gas both noble and rare belongs most intimately to her own streets. Although Las Vegas and Tokyo both have more ostentatious neon than Miami, and Paris long ago enfolded the bright gas into the evening cascade of her amorous boulevards, no city does neon with Miami's style. Mere days after the Rodriguez invention was unveiled, Miami's salt-free vehicles had begun to glow with the same radiance that nuzzles its old Deco facades. A native Miamian muses to me that her city's neon must be a human signal back to the glossy subtropical landscape—a semaphore sent to roseate spoonbills, to pink flamingos and lurid sunsets—a friendly, natural wave, a wish to belong.

Soon after the debut at the Grand Prix, the neon effect began to migrate from South Florida westward to Texas and California. It moved northward up the Eastern Seaboard until it reached the Mid-Atlantic coast, where it began to bog down. In Maryland and Virginia, the effect was declared illegal, possibly because under-body lighting tends to wash out painted highway lines, possibly because the police are a jealous police. (Especially the police do not care for other vehicles using blue light, which is their own color.) Of all regions, New England has been slowest to respond; to find my peers I must travel to the warmer, Latin quarters of our city, undimmed by the flinty northern palette.

〜 〜 〜

Naturally, I am aware that a good many people are not only *not* putting neon on their cars, they have sold these cars and are going about on bicycles and subways, mentioning holes in the ozone layer. Who does not take their point? The automobile was once our super-dense icon of protean motion, of independence. Was once made sensible by vastness; was a soulful chamber, its highways songlines. It was deliverance for Okies driving through dust. And then its Faustian appetite overtook farmlands and estuaries, dissolved the city in sprawl, fumed the air, spurred malls and Valhalla Villages. The car and its beds of tarmacadam possessed planners to trade in the boulevards of memory for cloverleaves and concrete ramps. It has nearly ruined the railroads (our Zephyrs, Crescents, and Coast Starlights).

The usual erasure of places—all the vanishing places that can be carried only as Baudelaire's great swan carries its natal lake through the poultry market—has been painfully accelerated by the automobile's demands. I know that. And yet I wish to adorn the suspect thing. It is one of the small canvases of a fragmented people. I know that too. And there is a credibility problem here for me, who has for years railed about the Commodification of Everything, saying, Lookyhere, Marx was right, Marx was right, consumer culture does insidiously invite us to think of everything, even our very own lives, as "product." And yet I am gladly shelling out $154.99 for a box of high-grade glam. Perhaps it is because these underbelly lights, while admittedly not a totally worked-out policy for transformation of culture, seem finer, truer, more heartfelt than one president's let-them-eat-cake "thousand-points-of-light" non-program. Because the gonzo extraterrestrial fireflies feel like descendants of Baudelaire's *movements brusques* and *soubresauts*, the strange and quick new ways of moving in the city. Because they are nite lights, sending the kind of signals—"affectionate, haughty, electrical"—of which Walt Whitman spoke. We can easily guess that the poet of the urban world would go for neon lamps: "Salut au monde!" Whitman calls across the mobile century, "What cities the light or warmth penetrates I penetrate those cities myself . . . I raise high the perpendicular hand, I make the signal."

Maybe too it is because these glow pods are a shard of the sublime, the old aesthetic of exaltation, so chastened over this century by a well-known catalogue of horrors. Maybe the sublime has turned hyper-modern, calibrated its energies, and bolted the idea of ecstatic transport onto Trans Ams—is lurking underneath things. Maybe I shouldn't say much more. Maybe the ultimate effect is, after all, just fun and flash, a sassy way of saying "I'm here." But it turns a mass-produced object into a carriage of light, and the light these youths bring into the city also seems to work a little as safe passage, as a visa across the often guarded lines of urban and ethnic territory. *"Es como una familia,"* one young man will say of the fraternity of neon.

\|\|\| \|\|\| \|\|\|

About the time that our ground begins to relax into spring, Annie, the tango dancer, tells me about Bigelow Coachworks. Annie has a leonine shock of gold hair, a closet full of swirly skirts, and a collection of vintage Fiestaware. She dances the slow Argentine-style tango and I felt sure that her word about neon customizers would be trustworthy. The first thing I notice about Bigelow Coachworks (other than it being named coachworks) is that the shop is immaculate. Not one oil-soaked rag. Inside the office there is a counter and a young woman behind it whose strawberry blond hair has been teased and sprayed into what used to be called a beehive. For neon, the young woman says, I must talk with Jim Jr.

No sooner have I said the word "neon" than Jim Jr., who has the palest kind of amber eyes, has plunged into the issues: First, the switch and ways it can be wired — into the headlights or parking lights, or independently onto the dash. The independent switch is a problem, Jim says, because you can forget to turn it off and drain your battery. Next, do I want two tubes or four? Two is plenty in Jim Jr.'s opinion; in fact, having no rear-mounted tube avoids the messy matter of plastic cases melted by the exhaust pipe. Now the mounting. Am I aware that the tubes aren't really made for New England winters? And do I know that the kits don't come with dismounting hardware? Do I know that Jim has engineered custom clamps which stay in place and make it easy to pop the tubes in and out with the seasons? As for rust, a touch of silicon on each screw will suffice.

It is a virtuoso romp, all the nuts and bolts of the neon sublime known and mastered by Jim, who has installed some fifteen systems, including, he says with a shy smile, the one on his own truck. My man. Jim Jr. levels with me about the thirty-six-inch tubes.

"These are going to give a *lame* effect," he says, examining the kit. "There isn't enough *juice* here for the effect we want."

Fortunately, the fifty-four-inch tubes for the effect we do want can be had right up the street, at Ellis The Rim Man's Auto Parts store, a temple to the aftermarket product where a beefy salesman shows me the selection (all made by the Rodriguez brothers) and then says, in the tone of a man who wants to have a clear conscience,

"You know, it's really dying out."

"Dying?"

"I think the kids just got tired of being harassed by the police." The salesman now pauses, glances at the two young salesclerks at the counter, and clues me in: "It's only boys who buy this stuff— you know, ethnics, Hispanic boys."

As the present contradiction occurs to him, he studies me evenly.

When the young men at the counter see what I am buying, one of them asks politely, "Is this for your son?"

My son, I think, not the least insulted, only feeling the sudden sensation of having one, and being the kind of mother who would get a top-of-the-line neon kit for him.

"No, it's for me," I say, smiling.

"Al-*right*," the boys say, and shoot me the hubba-hubba look. Now they want to talk neon.

"*Sí, sí*," of course they have it on their *caros*. Enrique has green and José has aqua. They have neon *inside* their cars too—under the dash, on their gear shift knobs. The store has a demonstration model. José gets it out, plugs it in; we stand around it to ogle the colored coils zooming around inside the clear plastic handle.

What do Enrique and José like about having neon on their cars? What *don't* they like! It's way *chevere*, way cool, it's like being inside a nightclub! Man, it lights up your whole body and everything you go by, and makes things look really, really bright. When José and Enrique hear that I saw my first neon car near the store, they cry out in unison.

"That was *us!*"

"You drive a silver Camaro?"

"Oh, no" they cry again, just as pleased. "Oh, no, that *wasn't* us, that was Alberto. That's Alberto's spaceship!"

Now they want to tell me something way-way *chevere*: the festival is coming. That's where we can see all the best neon cars and also the low-riders slow-dancing their cars down the road, each spotless vehicle also booming with Salsa.

"So neon hasn't died out?"

"No way," gapes Enrique, incredulous at the thought. Wait and see! Much lighting-up in the streets before summer is over.

The boys hold the door as I exit the showroom—carrying a long cardboard box of glass, transformer, and rare gas under my arm. They step out with me onto the broad sidewalk of our city's Commonwealth Avenue. It is about nine at night, July, prime time, and while we are standing there a boy that Enrique knows comes billowing by in a Cougar with some brand-new magenta light to spill. He creeps almost to a stop.

"*Hola!*" he calls.

"*Hola!*" the boys call back. "*Que lindo se ve.* How nice it looks. *Que bufiao! Miraeso.* Look at that. *Ooouuu, la luz.*"

Sources and Suggestions
for Further Reading

MAPS

Groueff, Stephan. *The Manhattan Project: The Untold Story of the Making of the Atomic Bomb*. Boston: Little, Brown & Company, 1967.

Groves, Leslie R. *Now It Can Be Told: The Story of the Manhattan Project*. New York: Harper & Brothers, 1962.

Nobile, Philip, editor. *Judgment at the Smithsonian: The Bombing of Hiroshima and Nagasaki*. New York: Marlowe & Company, 1995.

Rhodes, Richard. *The Making of the Atomic Bomb*. New York: Simon and Schuster, 1986.

Sapirie, Samuel R. *A Secret Mission and Other Disclosures: Memoirs of the Manager*. Oak Ridge: Oak Ridge Community Foundation, 1992.

Smyser, Dick. *Oak Ridge 1942–1992: A Commemmorative Portrait*. Oak Ridge: Oak Ridge Community Foundation, Inc., 1992.

HYMN

Raboteau, Albert J. *A Fire in the Bones: Reflections on African-American Religious History*. Boston: Beacon Press, 1995.

Scales-Trent, Judy. *Notes of a White Black Woman: Race, Color, Community*. University Park: Pennsylvania State University Press, 1995.

225

WATERSHED

Boyer, Sarah, editor. *In Our Own Words: Stories of North Cambridge, Massachusetts 1900–1960*. Cambridge: City of Cambridge, 1997.

Brewster, William. "The Birds of the Cambridge Region of Massachusetts," *Memoirs of the Nuttall Ornithological Club*, no. 4. Cambridge: Nuttall Ornithological Club, July 1906.

Emerson, Ralph Waldo. "Art."

Emmet, Alan. *Cambridge, Massachusetts: The Changing of a Landscape*. Cambridge: The President and Fellows of Harvard College, 1978.

Greenfield, Michael and Igo Roizen. *Nature*, August 1993.

Hiss, Tony. *The Experience of Place*. New York: Alfred A. Knopf, 1990.

Howard, Jerry, editor. "Alchemy at Alewife." *North Cambridge News*, June 1995.

Krim, Arthur J., with the staff and consultants of the Cambridge Historical Commission. *Northwest Cambridge: Survey of Architectural History in Cambridge*. Cambridge: distributed by the MIT Press, 1977.

Mitchell, John Hanson. *Ceremonial Time: Fifteen Thousand Years on One Square Mile*. New York: Doubleday & Company, Warner Books Edition, 1984.

HOUSE

Ayulward, Anne, principal investigator. *Three-Decker Housing in the City of Boston: A Reconnaissance, Triple-Deckers*. Boston: Boston Redevelopment Authority and Boston Urban Observatory, 1974.

Tucci, Douglass Shand. *Built in Boston: City and Suburb, 1800–*

1950. Boston: New York Graphic Society, 1978. This is my source for much of the historical information on the triple-decker, along with Ayulward (listed above).

PLOT

Marcus, Clare Cooper. *House as a Mirror of Self.* Emoryville. California: Publishers Group West, 1995.

NEON EFFECTS

Morgenthaler, Eric. "That's No Spaceship, That's My Car." *Wall Street Journal*, August 23, 1993.

GENERAL

Tanizaki, Jun'ichiro. *In Praise of Shadows* (1933), translated by Thomas J. Harper and Edward G. Seidensticker. Stony Creek, Connecticut: Leete's Island Books, 1977.

Acknowledgments

To my surprise, this book, which I had believed was going to be about just one geographical place, my small neighborhood in North Cambridge, Massachusetts, taught me again how elastic must be the border around the place we call home. Our local river led to an ocean, the mom & pop store to Haiti, the land into the Ice Age. As geographical and temporal borders dissolved, other, less physical terrains also presented themselves as important aspects of home: places of memory and longing, vanished cities, possible Americas — and a shared family history. The Tobagan poet Nourbese Philip has perfectly described this phenomenon: "It often happens," she says, "to a writer engaged on a particular story . . . that another one is being written, below the surface — the sea of one story floating into another."

My first and deepest thanks then is to my family — to my mother and father, and my brothers, Andy and Partap Singh, who gave this writing their blessing and improved it in the course of many conversations. Encouragement and help also came from several cousins — Nancy Callahan, Wade Blackman II, Bill Johnson, and Temo Callahan, Jr. — and from my great-uncle, Artemas Killian Callahan, Sr.

Sustained creative support during the whole course of this writing came from two matchless avatars of letters and love, Peter Niels

Dunn and Barbara Hindley, and from my editor, Deanne Urmy, whose genius, unparsable, involves faith and doubt, sense and sensibility.

The essays were also read by Lynda Morgenroth, Katherine Jackson, Patricia Brady, and John Landretti, each of whom offered elegant suggestions, and were copyedited by Chris Kochansky, a surgeon-poet of English. The book benefited greatly from the official and unofficial good works of Jill Kneerim of the Palmer and Dodge Agency.

Many persons bravely agreed to appear in these pages. I thank them all, and wish to ask their forbearance for any errors of fact or interpretation—nonfiction being a genre that mostly reminds a writer again and again that the mind, and language itself, is a natural fountain of fiction. I am grateful to friends, family, and to a house called Edgemer, for several retreats that provided peaceful times to write.

The essay "Hymn" is dedicated to the Union Baptist Church of Cambridge, Massachusetts, and could not have been written without the contributions of Reverend Jeffrey L. Brown, Reverend Zina Jacque-Bell, Reverend Dr. Cheryl Townsend Gilkes, the congregation of Union as a whole, and in particular Dr. Grainger and Deaconess Esther Browning, Deaconess Lillian Allen, Deaconess Emma Nance, Dr. Sylvia Johnson, Sister Pauline Beckford, Sister Cecilynn Bent, Deaconess Jane Dietrich, Sister Alice Waith, Deaconess Pam Harding, Brother Philip Layne, Sister Doris Callender, Sister Charlotte Morris, and Sister Nancy Brothers.

Individual essays benefited from conversations with Jim Armstrong, Joe and Alice Bain, Emerson Blake, Stephanie Bothwell, Bill Borer and Marcy Wasilewski, Laure-Anne Bosselaar, Steve Chase, Ellen Jane Cheslak, Ed, Marie, and Oscar Cyr, the late Bill

(Tippy) Farrier, Toni and John Fiske, Patricia Greeson, Alice Harrington, Professor Paul Hoffman, Jerry Howard, Teresa Iverson, Joanne Kauffman, Jill Kneerim, Ed Norberg, Eric Pheuffer, Janis Pryor, Dick Seagar, Joan Swarms, Alex Strysky, Professor Karl Teeter, Shegeiko Uppuluri, the late Venuata Ramamohana Uppuluri, Ram Uppuluri Jr., Rosemary and George Warne, and Rosanna Warren.

Steady consideration and support came from my wonderful colleagues at *Orion* magazine: Emerson Blake, Morgan Dix, Amanda Gardner, Marion Gilliam, Laurie Lane-Zucker, Christopher Merrill, Aina Niemala, Christina Rahr, George Russell, Jennifer Sahn, and Peter Sauer. At Beacon Press, Amy Caldwell, Shannon Brennan, Sara Eisenman, Dan Ochsner, Margaret Park Bridges, and Colleen Lanick were generous with their talents. Janet Heywood at the Friends of Mount Auburn, Rene Little and Simon Doubleday at the Cambridge Historical Society, and Erica Bruno and Charles Sullivan at the Cambridge Historical Commission each opened their libraries to me. Readings of in-progress essays were arranged by the Examiner Club, the Museum of Fine Arts, Boston, the New England Aquarium, the Arlington Public Library, the Cambridge Historical Society, and the Blacksmith House. Other assistance has come from Dorothy and Peter Edward Dunn, Mark Wagner, Soren Ekstrom, Kathy Butler-Jones, Donna Brescia, Annie Grear, Jim Gutensohn, Chuck Eisenhardt, Mary and Alex Sproul, Alex Johnson, Andrea Cohen, Carolyne Wright, and Ande Zellman, who first suggested that I write about "that place you like, Fresh Pond."

To all of the above, and to Angela, wherever she is, my gratitude.